A CHRISTIAN JOURNEY

With Faith and Fortitude

notionpress.com

A CHRISTIAN JOURNEY

With Faith and Fortitude

IN THREE PARTS

AMELIA D KUMAR

notionpress
.com

Notion Press

Old No. 38, New No. 6

McNichols Road, Chetpet

Chennai - 600 031

First Published by Notion Press 2015

ISBN: 978-93-5206-293-5

TO

Mishaal and Graciana Kathryn

The two precious gifts from God

Foreword

A Christian Journey with Faith and Fortitude by Prof. Amelia D Kumar is a welcome addition to the Christian literature published in India. This precious book comes as a challenge to religious traditions in an unpredictable world of changes.

In the first part the author makes an earnest effort to explore the mystery of pain with great authenticity. She describes the challenges from the scoffing sceptics to prove the risen Lord Jesus Christ. The plan of God for the Church is that she should develop in purity and perfection, the second part asserts. With extensive scripture references the last part shows a way to break the worldly bondage set by Satan. While reading, I feel all the Biblical heroes of faith come alive. The life and ministry of our Lord culminating in the cross and the resurrection is set as a model of life here and here after.

The book ends with a long poem in free verse which is purely inspirational.

Let us make a loud bravo, join hands with the author and walk with Jesus. We have more to gain.

Rt. Rev. Dr. D. Pothirajulu

[Bishop, CSI]

"For we live by faith, not by sight."

II Corinthians 5:7

Contents

Part I

Lily of the Valley

Preface To Part I

Is there a life after death?
Does that world really exist?

The book's first part unravels the mystery hidden behind these questions. The answer comes as good news to the discouraged. After reading this, they will not feel abandoned or unloved. This exuberant good news, when received and cherished by the reader, will prove rewarding, because it speaks about the persecution a believer endures and the plan of God for such believers.

Most Christians are satisfied with the mere experience of salvation; they never step out to do anything for Christ. What place is reserved for them when they enter eternity? The message presented here comes as a prophetic warning to awake, put on their armour and be battle ready.

Some endure suffering at the hands of scoffers, and face extreme persecution for being Christians. They remain true to their faith in the midst of their trials and tribulations. They do not allow themselves to be entangled by the affairs of the world. Instead, like dedicated soldiers, they are keen to obey their commanding officer, Jesus Christ.

A soldier fights a good battle not for the sake of his wife or children but for the sake of his nation; it is for a noble cause. Similarly, these believers put up a brave fight against devils and redeem men from the jaws of burning hell. They are the martyrs who will be crowned on the coronation day in the celestial city.

This part of the book brings cheer, courage and encouragement to all who serve in God's army, and are ready to fight and establish the Kingdom of God, here on earth. Bravo! Young Barraks! Join the Christian journey. The Lord, our God goes ahead of you. The battle is the Lord's. You walk with Him only to collect laurels and distribute them among your co-labourers. Let your faith and the peace of God reign supreme in your life.

The Author

Lily of the Valley

Stiff-necked Scoffing Sceptics

"Blessed is the one who reads aloud the words of this prophecy, and blessed are those who hear it and take to heart what is written in it, because the time is near."

[Revelation 1:3]

This is the one important message we read in the Book of Revelation. It foretells Christ's final triumph over evil. The Lord, God, controls all events happening around us, and He shapes and reshapes history according to His plan. God has allowed evil, but He does affirm that He would not lose control over it. As God's glory is coming to fill the earth, evil is moving towards its own end. Believers therefore can find hope through faith in God irrespective of all earthly circumstances. This word of hope is given to all believers. No matter how things look or move, God holds charge of history, and good will triumph ultimately. This revelation gives us hope.

I wouldn't want readers to ask critical questions and look for mundane details. Instead, I wish them follow the main flow of thoughts presented here. I pray to the spirit of the Lord to lead them in their spiritual journey. The book of mysteries will no longer be hard to read or understand. It will help us to find God's plan and purpose in everything we do and in everything we aspire for. Those who have as much faith as little children have, can understand the content of this book easily and march on to fight a good battle as a soldier of Christ.

"Endure hardship with us like a good soldier of Christ Jesus. No soldier gets involved in civilian affairs; he never wants to please His commanding officer."

[II Timothy 2:3]

In my youth, I thought whosoever accepted Christ as their saviour would become children of God and would therefore inherit the Kingdom of God. It is not that simple, I learnt later. As I grow, a new revelation was given to me, which affirms the allotment of places for passive believers and active warriors who fought a brave fight for Christ. Because Christ himself has told His disciples:

"Trust in God, Trust also in me. In my Father's house are many mansions; if it were not so, I would have told you, I am going there to prepare a place for you. And if I go and prepare a place for you, I will come back and take you to be with me that you also may be where I am. You know the way to the place where I am going."

[John: 14:1-4]

Let us now take a closer look at the verse: "In my Father's house are many mansions." From the words 'many mansions', we derive the idea that there are separate dwelling places, which are being allotted to us according to the good fight we have fought on earth. For the Lord says:

"Behold I am coming soon! My reward is with me, and I will give to everyone according to what he has done."

[Revelation 22:12]

Not all are crowned and taken to the Celestial city or the Throne room in Heaven. Only those who partake in His suffering will have the right to be seated with Him. Did we bleed for His sake as He bled on the Cross? Did we receive wounds and hurts in warfare-physically, mentally and spiritually?

A good soldier is a bonded servant, committed to serve his senior officer, always. This is the reason why Christ asked His disciples to leave everything for His sake and be willing to carry the cross. Leaving the world for Christ is a great gain. St. Paul experienced it. St. Paul calls on Timothy to stand firm, overcome shame and hold on to the faith with a good conscience. To Peter, suffering is only temporary and it is to be endured for a while.

Do you suffer because of your being a Christian? Peter comforts such men.

You need not be surprised at the painful trial you undergo often. Instead, rejoice that you participate in the suffering of Christ, so that, when His glory is revealed, you may be overjoyed.

"If you are insulted because of the name of Christ, you are blessed, for the spirit of Glory and of God rests on you. However, if you suffer as a Christian, do not be ashamed, but praise God that you bear that name. So then, those who suffer according to God's will should commit themselves to their faithful creator and continue to do good."

[I Peter 4:12, 13, 14, 16 & 19]

"In fact, everyone who wants to live a godly Life in Christ Jesus will suffer persecution."

[II Timothy 3:12]

When Jesus told Peter the kind of death the apostle would die, he knew it was not going to be a fair experience. In addition, he would not be the only disciple to die a violent death. According to a Church report, Matthew was slain with the sword; Mark was dragged through the streets till he met with his end; Luke was hanged on an olive tree; James was beheaded; Andrew was bound to a cross, from where he preached till he died; Thomas was run through with a lance; Jude was shot to death with arrows; John who identified himself as 'the disciple whom Jesus loved' was banished to the isle of Patmos. According to tradition, he was submerged in a cauldron of hot oil. But he remained steadfast in Jesus' love. These reports conclude that they all endured persecution for the sake of Christ. All those who know the Lord and remember His suffering on the Cross respond to His invitation:

"If anyone desires to come after me, let him deny himself and take up his cross, and follow Me."

[Matthew 16:24]

Those who suffer with Him will also share the glory with Him - a life forever free of pain. It is a promise given by Christ.

Sceptics point out that this belief itself, in a way, is selfish. They taunt the believers with ridicule that the Christians always think of the 'pie in the sky'.

Yet another charge is levelled against them: A Christian does not bother to improve the present state of his living on earth but always lives in a world of fantasy. By creating a make – believe world of his own, he deceives himself and deceives others, the sceptics say. They charge that a Christian strives to seek solace and comfort in a world of imagination, rather than involve himself in the affairs of the world.

How are we to answer these charges? First, we will have to understand one hard truth: Things that look real are not real.

"For our light and momentary troubles are achieving for us an eternal glory that far outweighs them all. So we fix our eyes not on what is seen, but on what is unseen. For what is seen is temporary, but what is unseen is eternal."

[II Corinthians 4:17, 18]

A proverb says, "You can lead a horse to a water trough but you cannot drink for it." Taking the waters of life is a spiritual experience meant for the individual. Unless God gives spiritual enlightenment, one cannot easily understand this mystery. St. Paul writes to the saints of Ephesus:

"I keep asking that the God of our Lord Jesus Christ, the glorious Father, may give you the spirit of wisdom and revelation, so that you may know Him better. I pray also that the eyes of your heart may be enlightened in order that you may know the hope to which He has called you, the riches of His glorious inheritance in the saints, and His incomparably great power for us who believe."

[Ephesians 1:17-19]

Only during the prayer of a believer, the Lord will open his eyes. He opened the inward eye of his disciples and they could understand everything. Then He opened their minds to understand the scriptures (Luke 24:45).

The sceptics have to understand that the Lord's assurance is given to believers. Every trial in our life is tested and proved when we stand with patience and perseverance. We face troubles everyday but in the midst of troubles, we see His gracious touch. In other words, we go to the den of lions with Him who is able to shut the mouths of wild beasts. Thrown into a burning fiery furnace is indeed a dreadful ordeal. However, the word of promise is, *"I will be with him in trouble."*

Every day we face fierce trials and sorrows. They threaten to overwhelm us. What is expected of us in such crisis is to go through them with the Lord and enjoy the greater blessing that is kept in store for us. That is the reason why Jesus said on one occasion: *"In the world ye shall have tribulation; but be of good cheer; I have overcome the world."* (John 16:33). Yet, we do not face any situation alone. He is ever with us to comfort and support us. He acts as he promised. The verse, *"I will not leave you as orphans,"* (John

14:18) is most comforting to a soldier who wages a spiritual warfare with demons.

The Lord provides all spiritual blessings one after another: *"From the fullness of His grace we have all received one blessing after another."* (John 1:6). All that a believer needs for the journey to Heaven is faith, and it is abundantly provided.

Anyone who walks with the Rose of Sharon leaves the fragrance behind. One could easily follow a bearer of rosebuds. All God's people carry such a fullness of grace that everyone knows where they have been by the tracks they leave behind. People following this fragrance will rejoice in His blessedness. Peter encourages his readers to, *"Live such good lives among pagans that, though they accuse you of doing wrong, they may see your good deeds and glorify God."*

[I Peter 2:12]

In the last day, scoffers will come ridiculing and following their own evil desires. They will say, *"Where is this 'coming' He promised? However, they deliberately forget that long ago by God's word, the heavens existed and the earth was formed out of water and by water. By the same word the present heavens and earth are reserved for fire, being kept for the Day of Judgment and destruction of ungodly men."*

[II Peter 3:3-7]

The ungodly are ever seen chatting with one another. They do not understand that such ungodly chatter corrupts good manners. Moreover, they speak abusively against everything because they do not understand things with a spiritual insight. The scales are still on their eyes. As

Jude warns, they understand things by their instinct; these are the very things that destroy them. The Psalmist begins the opening section of his book by sounding an alarm to the people.

"Don't stand in the way of sinners. Don't sit in the seat of mockers."

Let him who is vile, continue to be vile – for what he loses is his own soul, about which he has bothered least. He who comes very soon comes with the reward to everyone according to what he has done. Prophet Isaiah has heralded the same news. All those mockers who taunt the godly and ridicule them will see the one coming with the clouds.

"...and every eye will see Him even those who pierced Him."

As a sign of mockery, the Roman soldiers who crucified Jesus stripped Him and put a scarlet robe on Him. They blindfolded Him and demanded Him to prophesy. They placed a crown of thorns on His head. They mocked at Him by kneeling before Him and addressed Him, *"Hail, King of the Jews."* He reached Golgotha, crossing the path of mockery. The men who passed by hurled insults at Him. They offered Him vinegar, when He was thirsty. Two robbers were crucified with Him. Even one of the criminals in that hour of crucifixion joined the crowd in insulting Him.

Such mockers and scoffers, seen two thousand years ago, are still seen in our midst taunting the believers with a tone of sarcasm and mockery. They mock at the innocent with lashing remarks. Is life, then, worth living and worth rewarding? The innocent always suffer but the wicked prosper. At times, the life of the wicked looks enviable. The innocent are deeply disturbed when they see the ungodly living in worldly prosperity.

"Therefore pride is their necklace; they clothe themselves with violence; they scoff and speak with malice. In their arrogance they threaten oppression; their mouths lay claim to heaven, and their tongues take possession of the earth."

[Psalm 73:6, 7, 8]

Their hearts are callous and their minds are full of evil conceits. What is the promise made to the godly? In the view of eternity, godly living is more rewarding and it is certain.

Hence, let us examine carefully as to how a Christian should respond to persecution. The painful trial a believer suffers is not something that is happening only to him. Many in history have died for their religious faith.

The story of St. Agnes of Rome, a virgin-martyr, tells us the type of persecution she endured for the sake of her newfound faith in Christ. Agnes was a beautiful Roman maiden and a devoted Christian. Sempronius, the son of a Roman army officer, was enamoured of her beauty and offered to take her as his wife; but she rejected his offer saying that she had an Ideal Lover, fairer than any earthly suitor. He learned that the lover of whom she spoke was Christ. He laid rich presents before her, but she rejected his proposal. In his rage, he sent her to be degraded in a place of infamy. The soldiers, in an act of insult and mockery, stripped off her garments. When thrown to such disgrace, she bowed her head and prayed. Her hair became like a veil, covering her whole person. Sempronus approached her with an evil desire, but he was struck with instant blindness and convulsions. In the midst of her own suffering, she prayed for her tormentor. Upon her prayers, he was restored back to health. A fire was made and she was thrown into it. She stood unharmed, while her executioners were slain by its force. The people were still clamouring for her blood. And she was then slain with the sword. After her death, she appeared to her friends with the lamb by her side, a lamb whiter than snow and said, "Weep not! Dry your eyes and rejoice with great joy; for me a throne is prepared by the side of Him with whom I am now united."

We marvel at the simple faith of this young girl who faced so many trials for the sake of her Jesus Christ. The reward she won in Heaven was the blessed seat assigned to her next to her Bridegroom.

"Come, I will show you the bride, the wife of the Lamb."

[Revelation 21:9]

Another story of persecution is recorded in the Book of Daniel. Shadrach, Meshach and Abednego were bound and thrown into a burning fiery furnace. They fell down, bound together. However, they walked in the midst of the fire praising God and were blessed by the Lord. According to the book of Apocrypha, those three Holy young men did not feel the heat of the fire; instead, they sang a song of praise:

"Blessed art thou, O Lord God of our fathers. Thy name is worthy to be praised and glorified for evermore, for thou art righteous in all the things that thou hast done to us. Yea, true are all thy works,

thy ways are right and all thy judgments truth; for according to truth and judgment didst thou bring all these things upon us because of our sins. For we have sinned and committed iniquity, departing from thee. And thou didst deliver us into the hands of lawless enemies, most hateful forsakes of God; And cause not thy mercy to depart from us; put us not to shame; but deal with us after thy loving kindness and according to the multitude of thy mercies. Deliver us also according to thy marvellous works, and give glory to thy name, O Lord." The angel of the Lord came down, smote the flame of fire out of the furnace, and turned the fire into a moist whistling wind so that the fire did not touch them.

The story of Judith records the brave deed of a young and beautiful woman. The world has not seen such a woman, both for beauty of face, and wisdom of words. Judith, the widow of Mamasse, put away her mourning dress and put on her garments of gladness to protect God's people. She stepped into the enemy's camp bravely, with a zeal to exalt the name of God Almighty. She stayed in the camp for three days, went out in the night into the valley of Bethulia, and washed herself in a fountain of water by the camp. Moreover, when she came out, she besought the Lord God of Israel to direct her way to the raising up of the children of her people. God gave victory to this woman by giving Holofernes, the chief captain in the army of King Nebuchodonosor.

"For she put away the garment of her widowhood for the exaltation of those that were oppressed in Israel."

[Book of Apocrypha, Judith 16:8]

When people step out with zeal to bring glory to His name, He, in turn, comes down to exalt His people. God is glorified in our sufferings. That is the reason why St. Paul boasts not of any other thing except his sufferings.

"That is why, for Christ's sake, I delight in weakness, in insults, in hardships, in persecutions, in difficulties. For when I am weak, then I am strong."

[II Corinthians 12:10]

The sceptics believe in the concept of the self-effort of man. 'Self-giving' is a true prayer for them. They think that in spiritual attainment, man should aspire to merge with the Divine. They say that man's constant aspiration of the self will be an effective means by which the soul can be turned fit to be in the abiding presence of the Divine. They go to the heights of calling themselves Gods by achieving glory to their names with all titles, wealth, intellectual ego, language supremacy, the light and the radiance of Lucifer ever glowing on their faces. They assure themselves that one can transcend to any great height through one's self giving. They raised questions:

Why should some be sacrificed as sacrificial goats and endure suffering?

Is there a meaning to a life in which all personal happiness of an individual is finally renounced?

How is it that a loving God demands or accepts such sacrifice and why?

The Christian answer is clear. All those who suffer unite their suffering with the sufferings of Christ on the

Cross. He willingly embraced this kind of death in order to liberate humanity from the yoke of sin and death and thereby, to bring about the reward of eternity in heaven.

But the scholar critics point out that it is we, not the Divine, who are in love with our sorrow. It is we ourselves who cling to pain because we cannot imagine a spiritual path that is not strewn with sharp stones. Humanity is enamoured of suffering, they say, and that is the reason why Christ still hangs on the Cross. They go to the extent or of ridiculing the Christians by saying that Christians turn suffering into something divine to make it a means of saving the earth. In other words, they argue that Christianity turns suffering into an instrument of the earth's salvation.

Their repeated tone of mockery ends thus in their final verdict: If Jesus was the son of God, he need not have suffered on the Cross but could have come down and saved Himself.

This tinge of sarcasm is not new to a Christian. The Jews uttered a strong cry when they saw the bleeding Christ on the Cross two thousand years ago.

The people stood watching, and the rulers even sneered at him. They said, *"He saved others; let Him save Himself if He is God's Messiah, the Chosen One."*

[Luke 23:35]

The passers-by reviled Him, shaking their heads, and saying, *"Save yourself! Come down from the Cross!"*

[Mark 15:13]

Thus, the world today ridicules Him for the suffering He endured on the Cross. It does not see beyond the death of Christ. But the Scripture does not stop with a dead Christ. The picture is extended to the resurrection scene, His appearance before the disciples, and His promise to send a comforter to His believers while being taken to the heaven.

The Heavenly Father did not want to leave the followers of His son as orphans. Instead, He sent the helper, the Holy Spirit, into their troubled hearts in the form of a Divine Spark, and cheered up their broken and contrite hearts. Therefore, suffering is no more a suffering to the followers. Their suffering is turned into joy. This word the 'Helper' in the original Greek is called 'Paracletos'. In English, it brings out the following meanings: advocate, comforter, consoler, counsellor, teacher, guide, helper and intercessor.

Hence, the Holy Spirit fulfils all the above-mentioned offices for the believers. The work of the Holy Spirit, therefore, is a living miracle turning suffering into joy! The world sees the tumultuous waves of a sea on its surface but not the calmness in its depths. Once, if the eyes of the intellectuals are open, then their hearts will burn with the flame of love and bring glory to His name.

Some religious beliefs talk of rebirth and the concept of man taking several forms of body at every birth. Of what use is the body when the soul has not undergone a surgery of rebirth? This rebirth is attained only when man has made a true repentance of his sins and gained a feeling free from guilt. This remission of sin is possible only with the holy blood of Jesus Christ.

A certain man saw his dead neighbour in his dream. The dead neighbour pointed at an angel with a trumpet who was standing by his side and told the man, "No one at my home seems to bother about Eternal life." The man understood the importance of the message. It was a message to be shared immediately with the dead man's wife and children. There was not a stir of excitement or joy when the message was shared with the wife. She said that the night when she was praying for her son, her husband passed away. She was praying for her wayward son with travailing agony. She had prayed not for her son's salvation but for his worldly exaltation.

What startled the man more was the woman's question, *"Were you reading any book about life after death that night?"* She had no mind to understand the message.

Sceptics are ever seen scoffing and ridiculing the message of God. People in this materialistic world expect the dead spirits to appear and tell them about the secret places of hidden treasures of gold. That would elate their spirit. Isaiah speaks about another treasure of riches:

"I will give you hidden treasures, riches stored in secret places, so that you may know that I am the Lord, *the God of Israel, who summons you by name."*

[Isaiah 45:3]

People are not interested in knowing about such treasures. Does not Jesus speak an end-time message of preparation for His coming? But what a complacent attitude man has towards the knowledge of eternity! All we can do is to bring them again to the remembrance of the words of Jesus:

"Behold I come quickly."

[Revelation 22:7]

"And behold I come quickly; and my reward is with me to give every man according as his work shall be."

[Revelation 22:12]

We are in Paradise

"Why are you here?"

"What are you doing?"

I asked.

"We are in Paradise."

We are still standing under the tree, came the reply.

One in the multitude answered. When he turned his face towards me to answer my question, I was taken aback and completely surprised. I see him after a period of several years. The person I had known on earth now seemed quite young and exuberant. He was dazzling in his white robes. He was the very picture of health and happiness. Those who stood around him were seen young in appearance. The lapse of long years has not made its mark upon them because a day in paradise runs to a thousand years of earthly existence. God has the power to reverse the aging process. As the Bible describes it: *Let his flesh become fresher than in youth; let him return to the days of his youthful vigour.* (Job 33:25).

Jesus spoke of this 'recreation' or 'renewal' of all things in Matthew 19:28

"I tell you the truth, at the renewal of all things, when the Son of Man sits on his Glorious throne, you who have followed me..."

The words 'still standing', uttered with a tinge of sadness in the tone, puzzled me. I sat up on my bed recalling my dream again. I could see fiery chariots moving hither and thither – all running at great speed. All of a sudden, a chariot slowed its speed and stopped near me. I saw a host of people moving towards it. I could hear the words uttered by someone, "This is the one who endured persecution for Christ's sake." The onrush of this crowd thronged round the chariot to see who he was. However, in a split second, the chariot moved fast towards another realm. Then the multitude dispersed and stood in groups. Henceforth I asked one in the group:

"Why are you here?

What are you doing?"

The reply revealed that they regretted something which they had failed to do on earth.

This is how I was seized of a necessity to write on this revelation of God-man's regrets and God's rewards. I thought that it was my first duty to induce spiritual hunger among God's children. I must stimulate healthy development in spiritual growth among the Christians, because it is essential in these last days. Moreover, I feel it as a great burden in my heart that a sincere worker in the Lord's Vineyard should not go discouraged in his ministry.

At present, we see there is a real hunger among many of us to study the word of God. This is a good sign of spiritual awakening that is taking place in all parts of the world. People show a new interest in the pursuit of knowledge of God and His eternal purposes and plans. I wish the reader would prepare himself to meet the Lord, who was once rejected, despised and crowned with thorns. He will appear as the Victor with all the brightness of His eternal glory; then every head will bow before Him and every tongue will praise Him, the Lord and God.

God's purpose and plan stand separate in relation to Time and Eternity. The human mind, in its mortal frame, cannot comprehend things that pertain to Eternity. However, everything is comprehensible in the sphere of faith. God's purposes and plans are revealed to man by the Holy Spirit. Jesus told his disciples, *"But when He, the Spirit of truth, comes, He will guide you into all truth. He will not speak on His own, he will speak only what he hears, and he will tell you what is yet to come… the Spirit will take from what is mine and make it known to you."* (John 16:13, 15).

"For we live by faith, not by sight."

[II Corinthians 5:7]

One can easily believe only when one enters the realm of faith with simplicity and innocence. We come across a beautiful picture of the resurrection episode and His first appearance, recorded in the Gospels. The re-entry of Christ was sensational and dramatic. At the end of the day, when the disciples assembled behind closed doors for fear of the Jews, Jesus came and stood in their midst. The disciples saw the hands and the pierced side of Jesus. They were glad that they had seen their Lord. However, Thomas, the doubting one, was not in the group. He was not willing to believe that the Lord appeared behind the barred doors when the eyewitnesses narrated the incident with great thrill and excitement. Many people boast of this type of unbelief as a mark of their intellectual superiority and power of reasoning; but their doubt is only a mark of a senseless heart and blurred vision. Jesus, because of His immense mercy, once again appeared before the disciples, after eight days. This time, Thomas was also present. Thomas was overwhelmed with great joy and sorrow, when Jesus asked him to touch and feel the nail prints on His pierced body. He could only say, *'My Lord and my God."* How much tears the disciples and Thomas would have shed, weeping aloud, when Jesus showed his bruised body lovingly and patiently. This was indeed, something marvellous. His Shekinah glory was transforming people.

In the unseen world, God's only son, Jesus Christ is the centre and circumference of all His purposes and plans. He has the 'keys of death and Hades'. The great multitudes in white robes are ever singing songs of praise. They praise Him who had redeemed us to God by His own blood. The underworld at the end of the earth's history will witness the most spectacular scene, when every tongue in heaven, earth and beneath the earth will confess that Jesus Christ is Lord.

Let us turn to the Old Testament for a clearer perspective of this concept: What is life after death? King David lived in an age when numerous wars were fought and a great number of people died at every battle. Hence, death was a familiar term. Yet, the puzzling question ever asked to one another was, *"What happens to me after I die?"* People wanted to get an answer to that question. Death, with all its horror, remained mysterious and frightening to everyone.

They called it 'Sheol', a dark and shadowy place, where dead people go. Sheol was the great leveller for the prince and the pauper, the poor and the rich, the powerful and the weak; it meant the end of man's plans and ambitions and an end that closes man's relationship with God. However, the Psalmist makes a bold declaration that God has power over the grave; he can redeem a person from there. Man's flesh will rest in hope in God's presence. God will not leave the soul of his chosen servant in hell; neither will he suffer his holy one to see corruption.

"Therefore, my heart is glad and my tongue rejoices; my body also will rest secure, because you will not abandon me to the grave, nor will you let your Holy one see decay."

[Psalm 16:9–10]

Jonah, who was in the belly of the whale for three days cried out in agony: *"He cried out of the belly of whale."*

[Jonah 2:2]

The womb of the whale was like 'Sheol' or 'Hades' for Jonah. Sheol, according to the Old Testament, is a dark and unseen world, a place meant for the departed human spirits. This is made clear by Jesus Himself in the New Testament. A number of scriptural references can be cited from Jesus Christ's statements about heaven and hell.

Heaven is a place of perfect happiness and eternal communion with God. Hence, Jesus advises people to store up treasures in heaven. He asks us to take our inheritance to the kingdom He had prepared for us since the creation of the world. St. Paul presses on towards the goal to win the prize for which God called him heavenward in Christ Jesus. Many live as enemies to the cross of Christ.

"Their destiny is destruction, their God is their stomach, and their glory is in their shame. Their mind is on earthly things. But our citizenship is in heaven."

[Philippians 3: 19 – 20]

Man, after his long day's journey in this wilderness of chaos and confusion longs for a place of rest and peace. That kind of happy conclusion is given in the Book of Revelation. Heaven assures us of a new order of things. Ten thousand bright angels in glory, dressed in white raiment so fair, are ever seen singing and shouting, *"Hosanna."* All our toil and gloom of the desert life will be over. The flowers will bloom on forever and the leaves of the trees will be evergreen. There will be no night in the celestial city for it is brightened by the Lord God Almighty and His son Jesus Christ.

"The city does not need the sun or the moon to shine on it, for the glory of God gives it light and the lamb is its lamp."

[Revelation 21:23]

As we stroll in the garden of Heaven clasping the hands of our loved ones, our 'joy will be complete', as He promised. We shall ever hear the song of the redeemed in heaven. The heavenly kingdom is full of music without discord. The winding roads are arranged with exquisite taste by the Master Builder; His wisdom is profound; His power is vast. Lovely souls would move fast, saluting one another in a heavenly courteous way. Nowhere had we seen such bright and cheerful faces beaming with happy contentment. He shows to each one of us, our mansions, and we move in forever to stay there. Heaven is real to all those who have prepared themselves for it. The earth is the first habitation of man. Heaven is the future and eternal habitation of men who do not waver in their faith.

"Now we know that if the earthly tent we live in is destroyed, we have a building from God, an eternal house in heaven, not built by human hands. Meanwhile, we groan, longing to be provided with our heavenly dwelling… Now God has made us for this very purpose and has given us the spirit as a deposit, guaranteeing what is to come… I say, I would prefer to be away from the body and at home with the Lord. In the body or away from it. For we must all appear before the judgment seat of Christ, that each one may receive what is due to him for the things done while in the body, whether good or bad."

[II Corinthians 5: 1- 4; 7 – 10]

Everything in Heaven will enrapture us with delight. We shall be entranced by the beauty of the mansion. Our sacrifices on earth are little when compared to the great gains we receive there. The Biblical verse mentioned above will enrich our understanding.

"For our light and momentary troubles are achieving for us an eternal glory that far outweighs them all."

[II Corinthians 4:17]

God has thus made two worlds for man. While in body, he is for the physical world, and out of the body he is for the spirit world. When man dies, his spirit, that divine spark, is separated. Spirit does not mean 'ghost' as many misinterpret. It is a body in spirit. John, on the island of Patmos, on the Lord's Day was on the Spirit, and he heard behind him a loud voice like a trumpet. John, in spirit was fully conscious of the place where he stood. He was able to exercise his faculties, feel emotions, recall things from memory, and admire beauty around him. He was struck with bewilderment at the sight of the bright lamps.

I was once carried in the spirit and was shown Paradise, in my dream. In my spirit form, I could exercise all my faculties. I enjoyed the sight of evergreen trees loaded with fruits. The sweet fragrance of those heavenly flowers filled me with excitement. I saw a great multitude of people standing under the trees and conversing with one another. We hear words through our ears, while we are in body. A special device of comprehension was felt possible here, without taking any effort to hear. An audible voice was heard distinctly in my inner consciousness.

This concept of conversation is beautifully brought out in the story of the rich man and Lazarus. Jesus was narrating this story. He was sharing a great secret with people, about the existence of Heaven and Hell. This story is recorded vividly by Luke in the sixteenth chapter. Jesus was narrating something, which He knew really happened in the other world. The bodies of the rich man and the poor man, Lazarus had been buried. The rich man, being in torments in hell, sees Abraham afar off and Lazarus in his bosom. The abode of the righteous is described by Jesus as 'Paradise' and 'Abraham's bosom'. When the blessed are dead, they bid farewell to their body, and they are comforted in Abraham's bosom.

One more reference can be cited here, from the book of Luke. One of the criminals, hanging on the cross, hurled insults at Jesus. However, the other criminal rebuked him saying, *"We are punished justly, for we are getting what our deeds deserve. But this man has done nothing wrong." Then he said, "Jesus, remember me when you come into your kingdom." Jesus answered him [the penitent thief], "I tell you the truth, today you will be with me in Paradise."*

[Luke 23: 40 – 43]

Scripture, therefore, teaches us that life does not terminate; it is a continual process. A great gulf separates the saved and the lost. The righteous are to step into Paradise and the wicked to be thrown into the lake of fire. A man by his natural senses does not understand this because he judges everything from outward appearances. However, for a spiritually born again Christian, the invisible things are of eternal value. He does not fix his eyes on what is seen, but what is unseen; for what is unseen is eternal.

Again, Scripture throws more light on the change of abode of the righteous. This is because Jesus rose from the dead and ascended to the place of His original glory. Apostle Paul speaks of a certain man in Christ and his experience of going to Paradise, where he heard inexpressible words, which were not lawful for men on earth. Paradise is explained as the 'third heaven' by him. In the narration of the story of the rich man and Lazarus, only a 'great gulf' separated the saved and the lost. However, by the resurrection of Jesus that paradise is now in the immediate presence of God.

This is Paul's message to Ephesians: *"When Christ ascended on high, He led captives in his train and gave gifts to men."* (Ephesians 4:7). He who ascended on high, also descended to the depths of the earth. When He returned from there, He did not return alone. He led a multitude of captives with him. In completing his great work of redemption, he brought back all the occupants of the Paradise division to the immediate presence of God. This great gift was given to humanity since Jesus Christ had borne all our sins on the Cross, died and was resurrected. Without His resurrection, there is no heaven for the righteous.

The very region of the Saved is now changed. The 'underworld' and the 'third heaven' are situated apart. Therefore the spirit world no more frightens us. Death is no more a mystery bringing thoughts of horror to a born again Christian. Every Christian desires, like Paul, to depart from this body so that he can be present with the Lord.

"I would prefer to be away from the body, and at home with the Lord."

[II Corinthians 5:7]

The great fear of death is conquered by Christ on the Cross!

In the books of Isaiah (61) and Luke (4), we come across the great mission that was assigned to the Son of God. One of the main purposes for which the Son of God was anointed is 'to preach deliverance to the captives'. His act of descending into the lower depths applies deeper significance when he redeemed the captives and enabled them to stand before the Throne of Mercy.

Though such a change is brought in the abode of the righteous, yet they too have to avail the day of resurrection. God's word guarantees: *"There is going to be a resurrection of both the righteous and the unrighteous."* The wicked in Hades wait for the day of resurrection. The resurrection of the righteous promises them hope and therefore they are ever cheerful. However, to those who are 'lost', it brings a dread of terror. The wicked are destined for eternal torment for ages. 'Lake of fire' is their ultimate land in which they land finally. They will be 'in danger of the fire of hell', as Jesus himself says. The thought is terrifying more because the place is described as the 'place where worm never dies and fire never quenches'. What does the book of Apocrypha say about the punishment? *"Woe to the nations that rise up against my kindred! The Lord Almighty will take vengeance of them in the Day of Judgment, in putting fire and worms in their flesh; and they shall feel them and weep forever."*

[Judith 16:17]

To some, acceptance of Jesus Christ or Immersion baptism looks like the grant of a passport. They do not want to share the experiences of those who have received water baptism. They hide it as a great secret because circumcision is not in their hearts. A truly saved person will run and share the joy with the whole world.

Everyman is promised of salvation when he calls on the name of the Lord. *"Everyone who calls on the name of the Lord will be saved."* (Romans 10:13).

This salvation experience delivers him from all evil habits. Rebirth is especially deliverance from things that separated people from God. Salvation is free, a gift to all who believe. It is God's wish that no soul should be perished in the burning hell. That was the reason why He gave His only begotten son to be crucified as an atoning sacrifice for the redemption of humanity. Hence, everyone can enjoy the eternity of heaven if he extends his hand to receive this gift of salvation.

However, many who are saved do not step out to grow spiritually. One should eagerly desire for gifts that are more spiritual. The fruit of the Spirit is love and joy. Love, in the real sense, means to love God with one's might, heart and soul and love his fellow beings for the sake of Christ. Joy means the joy experienced while enduring persecution for the sake of Christ. Because a life in heaven is the reward. Moreover, it is mainly dependent upon the work of a saved one on this earth. It is dependent upon bearing fruits of the Holy Spirit. Our unselfish service for Christ and men are recorded in the book of life.

Going to heaven through salvation experience is not a reward but a gift. God by His immense grace has allotted us a place in heaven but it is only a gift and not a reward. Then who are the winners of reward? Those who lived a life with faith in Jesus and those who did His work in saving others are the winners. We are saved to save others. We must serve others when we are saved by God. Such acts decide the place we shall occupy. The moment Jesus lifted us from sin, He infused the thought of heaven in us. We select our own grade of mansion in heaven. We are thus rewarded according to the words we speak and the deeds we do. We shall be acquitted or condemned by the words we speak. Our words and work on earth determine our reward and place in heaven.

We shall all stand before the judgment seat of Christ and every one of us shall give an account of himself to God. We are not saved by our righteous acts but by His sheer grace. Our reward in heaven is decided by the work we have done for Christ, here, on earth. We shall give account of our deeds done in the body from the day of conversion.

'For we must all appear before the judgment seat of Christ, that each one may receive what is due to him for the things done while in the body whether good or bad."

[II Corinthians 5:0]

Paradise is the place of introduction for souls. As soon as they reach the portals of paradise, everything is brought to Light. The Holy Spirit convicts them of their sin and points out their wrong deeds. The Light that travels from the throne of God fills all the places – the Throne Room, the Celestial City and the Paradise. The Light brings all the works of the new arrivals to their remembrance, since the day of their conversion. They realize that their work was built of weak materials like straw and stubble. When fire tests his or her work, every believer comes to understand that his work was not built on the solid foundation of Jesus Christ. The believer, who was passive here on the earth, is thrown to shame when he looks around – the beauty of the scenes around him. He begins to regret that he did not do anything good for the glory of Christ. He remembers those days when he lived bringing disgrace to His name. He failed to give words of cheer and encouragement to lonely and depressed souls. He never offered prayers for others. There were opportunities give, to share his testimony with the lost. However, his heart was callous. The moment he realizes that he has landed in a teeming, bright, and fertile land, he is deeply hurt inside. His heart is filled with remorse. He recalls those faces of captives who with their bowed heads and broken hearts stood in great anguish for deliverance. They stood like the bruised reeds; they were like the wick of the lamp that was about to be extinguished. They could have been delivered from their bondage by the mere prayers of the saved one. Those who are saved never took up prayers for them. Therefore, they are filled with shame that they have not done anything great for Christ.

With sorrowful eyes, they see that exquisite place which is reserved for them; they feel that they are unworthy. In fact, they long to come back to the earth and do service for His glory. Most of the born again Christians are motivated by others to work, which is almost like social service based on good intention. Any kind of Martha-like activity is valueless when it is not combined with Mary-like spiritual aspiration. We need to live our lives with a proper blend of contemplation and action. Many are prompted to do work for Christ with a selfish motive. Such selfish motives and intentions shall be burned easily.

A born again Christian receives a reward when he totally accepts the will of God with serenity, starting the work of the day assigned by Jesus and guided by the Holy Spirit. He does everything in love and unselfishly for the sake of Jesus and the good of others. The result of his work may bring joy or sorrow, yet he does it for Christ's sake. Such a sincere work of a Christian will not be burnt by His fire.

All kinds of moral activities done with good intentions, Martha-like services, faithful church attendance and our self-righteous acts bear no value as far as the reward in heaven is concerned. The souls thus undergo a period of regret for their earthly acts. Things that hinder their life in heaven are all washed away in the purifying waters of paradise. The waters flow from the throne room. The moment a soul of man enters the gates of paradise and opens his eyes upon the glory before Him, he falls prostrate upon his face with the deep feeling of praise for the present and regrets over the past. He is greatly bewildered over the glory of the land and regrets that he is unworthy to receive such a gift. However, once they are washed by the waters that come from the throne room they are happy.

The saints in paradise assure them with soothing words. "You are saved; Think not of your past. What God has forgiven He remembers no more." Many saints spend much of their time about the threshold of paradise and assist all who enter. The soul makes a clamorous cry, *"Am I acceptable to God; will He receive me?"* They are sure to enter the city of glory and light when they prepare themselves. They are instructed that they must not be restless or neglectful when they tarry under those trees. Those leaves have healing powers. They are instructed well to obtain all Christian graces. The trees will impart light, life and grace to their souls. When they press the leaves to their nostrils and bind them to their heart, no taint of evil will abide in them. Nothing impure will enter the celestial city.

"Then the angel showed me the river of the water of life, as clear as crystal, flowing from the throne of God and of the Lamb down the middle of the great street of the city. On each side of the river stood the tree of life, bearing twelve crops of fruit, yielding its fruit every month. And the leaves of the tree are for the healing of the nations."

[Revelation 22: 1 – 2]

Again, a verse from Ezekiel throws more light on the healing power of the leaves: *"Fruit trees of all kinds will grow on both banks of the river. Their leaves will not wither, nor will their fruits fall. Every month they will bear, because the water from the sanctuary flows to them. Their fruit will serve for food and their leaves for healing."*

[Ezekiel 47:12]

Water baptism on earth foreshadows the dip in the purifying waters of paradise.

Water stands as a powerful symbol signifying the death of the old man, his self, the man of sin, and the man of the world. There takes place a total transformation in him. A new man comes out of the water. By walking in the newness of life, he becomes a citizen of the heavenly kingdom. Man's earthly imperfections are fully washed and gone forever in this immersion in the waters of paradise. Out of the waters, he is brought to live with Christ.

Some of them accepted the Lord as their saviour but they never sought the Lord nor tried to know His will. They were satisfied with their own self-righteous acts. They slighted God and His righteousness. Their dependence was on their own merits. *"All their tears will be wiped away,"* it is stated. But I saw him answering with a tinge of sadness. Through the Holy Spirit, I understood the reason for their sadness. It was a happy and holy place. Some of them on earth were graciously endowed with gifts but they never made use of those talents for the glory of God. Gifts are given to draw souls to the kingdom of God. Those who enjoyed superfluous wealth did not spend it wisely for the harvest of souls.

Some reach paradise even before their appointed time. They reach in a hurry and regret in leisure. They know the fact that they have left their wives and children to struggle as widows and orphans in an unfriendly and hostile world. They know that even to maintain the bare necessities of life on the earth is a Himalayan task for their widows and orphaned children. Then they delight over their entry into paradise, because at a hairbreadth narrow point they escaped hell. At the same time, they weep over their mistakes and neglected opportunities on earth. As they sing songs of praise, they are rejoicing through their tears.

I mentioned at the outset that the person who answered me threw me into a series of surprises. I mentioned that he was known to me. He was my husband whom I lost years back. After his salvation experience, he was never seen working for the Lord. His chase after the world and worldly possessions could not be stopped by me. At a critical time,

I had to give up the course of his life to God's will. He met with a sudden death and I crossed a valley of tears for six long years.

In the same dream, I saw the soul of a martyr, taken in a chariot speedily to the city of glory. I just heard the words uttered that he was the one who suffered martyrdom for Christ's sake. His suffering on earth was intense. But it was soon over and he was immediately taken into the land of glory. He followed the words of the Lord:

"Fear not them, which kill the body but are not able to kill the soul, but rather fear him, which is able to destroy both soul and body in hell."

[Matthew 10:28]

We have heard so much of the days of awful persecution; thousands and thousands were killed by sword and fire. Nero, the neurotic had a peculiar way of persecuting the saints. He smeared the naked bodies of saints with tar and burnt them as midnight torches for his banquet hall. Their agonizing cries were music to the ears of that half-crazy emperor.

Many saints had suffered untold moments of anguish and agony. They walked in the valley of tears. They endured torture in prison. Saint Paul, throughout, suffered for Christ. Some of them were torn to pieces by wild beasts in the arena of amphitheatres for the amusement of cruel tyrants. Samson and David had trials of cruel mocking and beatings. Many ended their lives behind prison bars. Some had been stoned, some sawn asunder to pieces, or slain with sword. They had wandered about in sheepskins and goatskins staying in deserts and in mountains and dens and caves of the earth. Nearly all the apostles courted persecution with a willingness of heart. We recall the verse from Saint John's remarks:

"I saw the souls of them, who were beheaded for the witness of Jesus and for the word of God, and which had not worshipped the beast neither his image, neither had received his mark upon their foreheads, nor in their hands; and they lived and reigned with Christ a thousand years."

[Revelation 20:4]

There comes another reference to the trees of paradise in the Book of Revelation:

'To him who overcomes, I will give the right to eat from the tree of life, which is in the paradise of God."

[Revelation 2:7]

"To him that overcometh will I give to eat of the tree of life that is in the midst of the paradise of God?"

[King James Version Revelation 2:7]

"I shall grant the victor to eat from the tree of life that stands in the paradise of God."

[New Berkeley Version]

No pain is sent without a Purpose: It is confidential

In the previous pages, we have seen how the believers endured persecution for the sake of Christ. Let us now examine some of the notions behind the idea of suffering.

According to the existing concept, good people prosper and bad people suffer. Job's friends reasoned that Job must have committed some great crime and hence God was punishing him. They admonished him that his hidden sin had brought him to a state of calamity. They asked him to repent for his sin. They believed that a just God punishes man for his sin and a loving God forgives and restores man when he repents for his sins. Job believed in a loving God; Job also believed that God knew he was innocent. God's voice, heard in a whirlwind, dismissed this argument and rejected his three friends. God accepted Job and asked him to pray for the deliverance of his friends. Therefore, from the story of Job we infer that suffering does not result from a person's sin. An innocent man like Job also suffers for a period. We cannot reason out the specific cause why a person is suffering. It is recorded in the book of knowledge that God reserves that knowledge for himself. When anything unfair happens to us in our lives, it is good not to trace the reason but to accept it with a joyous spirit. For, we are asked to thank God for everything that happens in our life. All things work together for the fulfilment of God's plans. *"And we know that in all things God works for the good of those who love him."* (Romans 8:28)

Even the most difficult experience in our lives can be used in God's overall plan for good. Do good people see only good things in their lives? God, in the books of the Old Testament, promised His people success, protection and prosperity. It was a special covenant relationship made between God and the Israelites. However, Christians today cannot simply turn to these promises of prosperity. A closer look at the words of Jesus will throw new light on the covenant made between God and man in the New Testament.

Christians meet with accidents. They do suffer from fatal diseases like cancer. They lose their children at the prime of youth. They live in poverty and die in starvation. Do such things bring glory to God's name? The answer to such a question is, *"Yes."* Jesus promised certain rewards for Christians, but he also predicted poverty, rejection and persecution. Deuteronomy concept is to do good to others and get God's blessings.

"Your basket and your kneading trough will be blessed. You will be blessed when you come in and blessed when you go out. The Lord will grant you abundant prosperity in the fruit of your womb, the young of your livestock and the crops of your ground — in the land he swore to your ancestors to give you."

[Deuteronomy 28:5, 6, 11]

The rewards Jesus promised were the rewards in Heaven, but poverty, rejection and persecution are also the allotted portion to a believer here on earth. Many Christians have lived through poverty and persecution. Some have died as martyrs. For all these faithful Christians, the real rewards wait in their Father's land. The Israelites were good when they were in the desert, depended on God for their daily survival. However, once they reached the promised land of prosperity, they forgot God. The lush green landscape, full of streams, orchards and valuable resources gave them abundance. They credited every success to their own effort. They never gave glory and praise to Jehovah who blessed them abundantly. The cry of Moses *"Remember your God who liberated you from the hands of slavery of Egypt"* was thrown to the winds. This was predicted by God himself: *"When I have brought them into the land flowing with milk and honey, the land I promised on oath to their forefathers, and when they eat their fill and thrive, they will turn to other gods and worship them, rejecting me and breaking my covenant."*

[Deuteronomy 31:20]

We do not think of God when things move smoothly to our advantage. However, we turn to God when we are in trouble. Therefore, believe that it is our suffering which brings us closer to God. Jesus endured the cross for the joy that was set before Him. The very cross we endure will take us to the land of joy. Our earthly father or a teacher disciplines us because he loves us. Similarly, God disciplines us for our good. No discipline seems pleasant; at that time it is painful. *"Later on, however it produces a harvest of righteousness and grace for those who have been trained by it."*

[Hebrews 12:11]

Sorrows are so precious that they should not be wasted. Instead of allowing them to mend us, we allow them to mar us. We come across disappointment, pain, loss, loneliness, ill health or similar afflictions in our daily lives. These factors send us nearer to God. One great man of God has rightly said that sorrows will, if we let them in, *"Blow us to His breast as a strong wind might sweep a man into some refuge."* Hence, God's people can thankfully attest that they are brought closer to God by sharp sorrows, rather than by long days of prosperity.

Three kinds of suffering bring about much pain and discomfort to the believer. Physical pain is the result of disharmony between one part of our body and the rest. Physical suffering dampens the inner spirit of man. However, some of them have overcome their handicaps. John Milton was able to write his epic, Paradise Lost when he was blind. Physical handicaps have turned out to be great blessings to many believers. Edison could have had his hearing restored by an operation. His deafness in a way shut out the noise of the outside world and made him listen to the voice of the inner man. This enabled him to concentrate more on his research work. Helen Keller who was deaf, dumb and blind was able to overcome this triple handicap easily by relying more on God's help. She rightly says, *"It must be that when the Lord took from me one faculty, He gave me another, which is in no way impossible. When God shuts a door, He opens a window."*

Mental suffering is more painful than a physical ailment. Certain happenings around us can easily produce mental anguish. Paul experienced 'fear and trembling' and 'anguish of heart'. Mental agony is more intense than physical suffering because we can share our experiences of physical pain with everyone we meet. However, the mental torture that one is inflicted with cannot be expressed in words. When this untold agony is accumulated, it saps away one's energy and happiness.

Spiritual suffering is the worst of all pains as the spirit inside is grieved because of the negligent attitude we have towards the allotted duties of our God. A believer is chosen to further the work of the Lord by prayer in the quiet of his closet; but he often neglects it, running to please the world and people. Instead, if he or she had prayed, it might have resulted in more blessings to others.

Let us ask this question as to why a Christian should suffer. Our motto would be this: because our Lord Christ suffered, we Christians are ready to suffer. *"I will suffer too."* The Bible says, *"But the God of all grace, who has called you to His eternal glory in Christ, will, after you have suffered a while, make you perfect: He'll equip, stabilize, strengthen and firmly establish you."*

Satan may bring suffering but it has an end. God will use it for our good.

"The God of peace will very soon crush Satan under your feet."

[Romans 16:20]

Suffering, thus, has two sides, like a coin. First, suffering comes from God to bring out the best in us. On the other hand, Satan uses the same temptation and suffering to bring out the worst in us. Paul advises us to commit our pain and suffering to God because God who is mighty can work out all things for our good and His glory. God meant everything unto good. Pain is a blessing, for its repeated blows chisel us into fair proportions and beauty.

I know a couple who had a mentally challenged child. They lost all hope in life. They always wanted to find out the reason behind their suffering. When they discovered why they were put through such suffering and humiliation, they began to use all their talents in doing God's ministry. First, all that they could do was to pray for others. They now found a new meaning in their life. They realized that God comforted them when they comforted others.

Tribulation leads to patience, patience gives experience and experience offers hope.

We must have maturity to accept all such tribulations as one of the means to accomplish His purpose in us. We must stop showing a mournful face to God, and start showing Him a bright and cheerful face in the midst of tribulation! *"If God ploughs the field, he has a plan to sow seeds in it,"* says a proverb.

Does pain have a purpose? Just as the birth of a baby brings joy after the mother's labour pains, suffering for Christ brings forth more fruits. The branch of the tree that bears fruit is trimmed and pruned often to bring more fruits. If we allow suffering to accomplish its purpose, it can bring patience, knowledge and maturity in our thinking. Job was always true to the Lord, but the devil pointed out that it was all due to the material blessings that the Lord bestowed on him. God here uses suffering to prove that his chosen man, Job loved Him more than the material things of the world.

No one would wish to be persecuted. Our natural eyes will not find happiness in persecution. We all long for the fellowship of our neighbours. However, the more the hate and enmity we receive from the world, the more we walk closer to God. The animosity of the world is a valid proof that we are identified with our beloved Lord. Quite often, when we stand firm for the sake of righteousness, it would arouse the wrath of the world. Jesus had already warned the disciples that they should not be disappointed if the world hates them. *"And ye shall be hated of all men for my name's sake; but he that endureth to the end shall be saved."* (Matthew 10:22)

Once we decide to live for Christ, then we will have to suffer. St. Paul advises Timothy to live a godly life for the sake of Christ. Godliness, in turn, will invite persecution.

"All that will live godly in Christ Jesus shall suffer persecution."

[II Timothy 3:12]

People who suffer for Christ are often considered as misfits in this world. This world is an alien land to a true Christian. He moves about like a pilgrim or a stranger in the world, because 'our citizenship is in heaven'. (Philippians 3:20).

We see spiritual warfare wherever we turn. Satan brings in all kinds of weapons for our destruction. 'Discouragement' is a weapon aimed at believers. We should not be entangled with the affairs of the world. Instead, we should discern the devilish force that is working at the back of our opponent. Whoever lives godly in Christ shall suffer persecution. In the spiritual realm, we fight against the rulers of the darkness of this world. Darkness, we all know, hates light.

At the beginning of my own spiritual warfare, I was looking at problems through my worldly eyes. Within a short time, I could understand the work of the devil behind it. The moment I identified its nature I was able to bind its fierce nature using the mighty name of Jesus Christ. The devil came with all fierceness to attack me, but the Cross of Jesus with its brightness went before me and saved me.

When I taught my children to praise God for everything, the devil could not have its firm footing.

On one occasion, when the ferocity of the devil was very severe, I tried endlessly to tame its fierce nature, in vain. I even planned to run away from the scene and settle down somewhere. However, before leaving I undertook fasting and prayer for three days. It was my only weapon against the devil. When I finished my fast, I learnt the great lesson of discerning the types of devils men face. Then I bound those qualities, in the mighty name of Jesus Christ. Many souls were won for the glory of Christ. What are the weapons in this spiritual warfare? Jesus himself has shown us the secret of success in this spiritual combat.

"Therefore, He has said, "This kind can come out by nothing but prayer and fasting."

[Mark 9:29]

Then the lion of Judah rouses up with zeal to fight the battle for us. Fasting is not a tool to twist the arm of God and make our Heavenly Father give us exactly what we want. We do not fast for a car or a new house. We fast to save the souls of our loved ones. We fast to set the oppressed free. This springs from the heart of God. Our expectancy is sharpened to see a positive result when we avoid food. God wants to feed His children but He does not wish to allow food to control our lives. Arranging a feast after Church service has become a fashion both in India and abroad. When the congregation falls to devour upon the dishes we are reminded of a verse that was told about the heathens:

"Their destiny is destruction, their god is their stomach, and their glory is in their shame"

[Philippians 3:19]

I see people around me sharing their new recipes with their friends. They are eager to know about the new and latest preparation of cakes and sweets than the Books of the Bible.

Once I travelled a long distance and shared my testimony in a church. People did not bother to find out that I had come all the way from India. Instead, they rushed to their tables with food packs. They were rather keen on filling their plates with God's plenty. However, a few came and talked to me about the testimony I gave. People in countries which enjoy prosperity are in such a new kind of bondages; they are made captives by the Food Idol. In our society, food has become a new God.

The moment we decide to take up fasting for three full days, like the one undertaken by Esther, then our fasting will tear down the strongholds of Satan. Fasting infuses faith in us. Fasting makes us spiritually strong to face life's battles. Fasting destroys the pride in us and gives us a broken and humble spirit. Thus, it helps us to conquer the evil thoughts in our carnal mind. 'Mortify the flesh' is our slogan. Once we crucify the flesh, we move to a different spiritual realm.

The scripture says, *"The mind of a sinful man is death; but the mind controlled by the spirit is life and peace."*

[Romans 8:6]

The very fact that some around us always find fault with us is a proof that we are identified with Christ and His wounds. Jesus took all the insults that were hurled against Him and now it is our turn to receive insults for His sake. Paul is delighted in being persecuted because he feels Christ is being glorified through him. He is happy to say that in such small ways he is allowed to share in the sufferings of Christ. Isaiah speaks about the servant of the Lord thus:

"...You are my servant, Israel, in whom I will display my splendour."

[Isaiah 49:3]

In another version, it is given: *"In whom I will be glorified."*

Therefore, it is a great blessing to His chosen ones. *"Blessed are they which are persecuted for righteousness sake: for theirs is the kingdom of heaven."*

[Matthew 5:10]

Why the embracing of the cross is called 'Passion'?

It is through suffering that Jesus won redemption for His bride. Where there is passion or intense love, there is a sacrificial willingness to suffer. Therefore, suffering gives immense joy. St. Francis of Assisi shares this joy with a fellow brother of his monastery saying that the real joy is in the way he endures suffering for the sake of His bridegroom.

On one stormy night during their journey, the two lost their way and so knocked at the door of a monastery. There came the Porter with a cudgel and beat them blue refusing to give shelter.

"The Porter comes out in anger, and drives us away with curses and hard blows; calls us bothersome scoundrels. He shouts at us, 'Get away from me, you dirty thieves, – you certainly can't eat or sleep here!' – And if we hear it patiently and take the insults with joy and love in our hearts, oh, Brother Leo, write that that is perfect joy! Above all the graces and gifts of the Holy Spirit, which Christ gives to His friends, is that of conquering oneself and willingly enduring sufferings, insults, humiliations and hardship for the love of Christ. We cannot glory in all those other marvellous gifts of God, as they are not ours but God's. But we can glory in the Cross of tribulations and afflictions, because that is ours."

(Quoted from the Lover and the Beloved by John Michael Talbot)

Our Lord promises that all the persecuted will be happy. *"Rejoice," He said and, "be exceedingly glad; for great is your reward in heaven."* (Matthew 5:12).

Happiness is a reward we get when we receive the things we longed for; but joy is when we do not get what we wished for. That is the reason why the Prophet Habakkuk closes his book with a song of praise in the midst of nothing in the pen, nothing on the vines or in the oxen stall.

"Though the fig tree does not bud and there are no grapes on the vines, though the olive crop fails and the fields produce no food, though there are no sheep in the pen and no cattle in the stalls, yet I will rejoice in the Lord. I will be joyful in God my Saviour."

[Habakkuk 3:17, 18]

Trials and tribulations oppress us from all sides. Such trials, when they are heavy, may disorient those who are weak in faith. They are also capable of taking us to great heights. Those who bless God in their trial shall be blessed by God through their trials.

These beatitudes reveal the secret of happiness. They contrast future joys with present sufferings. All of them are promises from the Kingdom of God. The prophets were all persecuted. Jesus advised his followers to be glad in hardship, and 'to leap for joy' when persecution came. He repeatedly tells us to rejoice in suffering.

The right motive that lies hidden behind the persecution will be rewarded at the right time. The motive must be for His sake… for His righteousness' sake. Some, on facing hardships, are thrown to self-pity and they label themselves as martyrs. In fact, the very sacrifice a follower makes for Christ must give him immense joy, because Jesus the bridegroom had already embraced the Cross of suffering with a passionate love for the redemption of His beloved. Whatever a bride suffers for her bridegroom gives her exceeding joy.

The promised benediction is the reward in heaven. Having seen the rewards of heaven with spiritual enlightenment, the believers will no more get frightened. Instead the persecuted have the stamp of courage on their faces and in their hearts. They join the company of prophets. What a royal welcome waits for those martyrs in the celestial city! His chosen ones live as true testimonies before people; people are redeemed through their sacrifices. They receive this great blessing here on earth.

Any pain we endure is not arbitrary or purposeless. Like childbirth, pain will lead us to a happy end. God reaffirms one last word of triumph - that the sufferings we have undergone will lead us one day to a good missionary outreach among all humanity. He shall send His chosen ones to the distant islands that have not heard of His name or seen His glory. Such people will proclaim His glory among the nations. They are the ceremonially chosen vessels, consecrated wholly to the Lord. He selects some of them to be priests and Levites.

God does not evince pleasure in punishing His people. He does everything to achieve His plans. He has a perfect plan and accordingly, he moulds us all. When he finds a flaw, he removes it, and once again reshapes it to the design of His choice. We should make a total surrender to His plans. Such holy vessels can be used mightily for His use. Only when the seal of an alabaster jar is broken, the fragrance from it begins to spread everywhere. In His hands, the bruised and the broken hearted can be of great use.

No more 'I'. Let us drive away that ego in us. Let the head be unscrewed, and all that 'I and I' are removed from the mind. All knowledge puffs up our ego whereas love builds us up. Moses had to remain in the wilderness for forty years to forget all about the knowledge he acquired in Egypt as a prince in the Pharaoh's family. He emptied all his princely qualities and identified himself with the sheep; all he could do now was to bleat like the sheep. He was feeling empty inwardly to admit the fact that he was a stammerer. God's power intervenes to fill up such empty vessels.

Some have not experienced pain in their lives. We see such people moving from victory to victory in all their worldly pursuits. They are free from the burden that is common to man. Pride is their necklace and therefore, walking arrogantly with puffed up pride is their way of life. Their pride is swollen as a balloon, filled with conceited thoughts. They scoff and speak with malice. They love to speak gossip and spread scandals. They enjoy wealth and abundance. They buy their health with their wealth. So what do we say?

"In vain have I washed my hands in innocence. In vain have I kept my heart pure. I have been punished every morning."

Their life looks enviable for a brief while but their end will be sudden. They will be completely swept away. Like a dream, they will vanish. In the light of eternity, godly living is always rewarding. *"If you are insulted, because of the name of Christ, you are blessed, for the spirit of glory and of God rests on you."*

[I Peter 4:14]

God's glory rests upon us when we acknowledge the fact that we are weak. His grace runs like a stream from His throne of mercy when we cry out in anguish, admitting our weakness.

God opposes the proud but he bestows grace to the humble. Therefore, the great secret of success in life is to present our dire needs at His throne of mercy. No more are we independent. We are dependent upon Him and His grace. God admits pain to teach us an important lesson about grace; we learn to lean on His strength for everything. We learn to live with our fellowmen as taught by Christ. We are not independent 'go-labourers', but we are interdependent 'co-labourers'. As long as ego is there, we always wish to be independent but once we humble ourselves, we seek help from others and help others. So if we undergo the path of grief, sorrow, suffering or pain in life that is the right time to seek and receive God's blessings. We desperately search for a solution to our problems; that is the time to expect a miracle in our lives.

The boat must be empty; such a boat receives a miracle; we toiled all day and night and we got nothing. Jesus got into the boat and the boat was full of fish. Jars must be empty without wine, only then can they be filled again. There must be famine. God's mighty hand intervenes mightily to feed a widow and her son. Five thousand people must be there without food for days; they had nothing except five loaves of bread and two fish. Such a situation was waiting for God's glory to be manifested. People, who reason out, argue with their superabundant intelligence that the boy would have carried a big fish that was able to feed five thousand. How ridiculous is their argument! A small boy carrying a whale and a bakery on his small head! These men never expect miracles and so they never believe in miracles. They go to the extent of arguing that the Israelites could walk on the road that was made in the Red Sea because the Red Sea had only knee-deep water. We tell them, *"Is it possible, then for the chariots of Pharaoh to get drowned in knee deep water?"* The statement of the drowning of Pharaoh's chariot is written in the Bible for such doubting sceptics. St. Paul makes an apt comment in II Corinthians 12:10.

"That is why for Christ's sake I delight in weakness, in insults, in hardships, in persecutions, in difficulties. For when I am weak, then I am strong."

A lover delights to suffer any affliction for the sake of his beloved, because she is the desire of his heart. How can we change things that are painful? The answer is found in St. Paul. We have to focus our eyes on the eternal. God has placed us here on this earth for an eternal reason. He uses the temporal to prepare us for the eternal.

"Our light affliction which is but a moment, worketh for us a far more exceeding and eternal weight of glory."

[II Corinthians 4:17]

The moment we turn our eyes from a difficult situation and turn to look on the eternal God, we are no longer in affliction. Out of painful things, we get certain good things. We are asked to cast our burden on to Jesus and believe that Christ is victorious in all things. He permits Satan to bring mischief in order that we may be His instruments to prove that Jesus never fails. Every situation that is permitted in our life is part of God's eternal plan. He has not asked us to close our eyes to reality. Indeed reality is that which God uses in all things for our good. In every difficult situation, he has asked us to praise and love God and our fellowmen. Praise and love are the two powerful weapons used in this battleground.

Praise is not just about feeling good. It is one of the dominant weapons in our spiritual warfare; the demons hear and tremble, the moment we start to praise. It is always the good who suffer most; this is often true, because they love

God and God in return loves them; therefore God's chosen ones are the constant targets of the devil's attack. He tries all strategies to deceive them and once he is defeated in his deceptive strategy he tries to wear them down and disables them in their physical or mental strength by his repeated attacks.

The soul of man is the battleground. The uncommitted areas in our mind are the most vulnerable areas for the attack of the devil. God trains us in a special way so that we shall serve Him with a genuine heart. He wants to use us, mightily, especially for the winning of souls. He gives permission to Satan to attack us so that we might see God's power in operation.

The fallen angels are still under the sovereignty of God, and God has set certain limits to their activities. When they want to go beyond, they have to seek God's permission. Jesus tells Peter that Satan requested him to sift Peter; yes, in the sifting process the good seeds are to be separated from the chaff. The chaff in us is to be removed and purified. God permits all of us to be exposed to this kind of process, so that we might come to know Him better.

Secondly, he wants us to empty all the doubt, unbelief and everything that hinders our faith. The Lord God wants us to grow more in faith. There is more to learn than we can possibly learn in this lifetime. How are we going to move mountains by faith, raise the dead, transport our bodies from one place to another and supply bread to feed thousands? Verse 20 in the third chapter of Ephesians says, "Now unto him that is able to do exceeding abundantly above all that we ask or think, according to the power that worketh in us." When do we get that power?

"Most gladly therefore will I rather glory in my infirmities, that the power of Christ may rest upon me!"

The power of Christ is released in our life when we believe in this. The very weakness that threw us into a state of defeat is changed into strength in that area. This is marvellous.

Soldiers in the army have to learn discipline first and undergo training before they are sent to fight in combat. Great is the call of God and therefore greater is the training the believers must undergo.

Sometimes we cross the path of pain where we violate God's law. For example, Abraham accepted Sarah's advice in bringing out his generation through Hagar, the handmaid of Sarah. It all ended in pain when he was once again in a position to listen to Sarah's advice. He had to drive away Hagar with his son Ishmael. Jacob, the deceiver of his father and brother, was in turn deceived by his Uncle Laban. God's blessing was poured into his life when he completed the period of punishment. Unrepented sin belongs to the territory of the devil. God withdraws his protection when He finds in us an area of unrepented sin. Our safety and victory are absolutely assured by our obedience to God. This total submission ensures protection and safety to us. The disciplining rod on Jacob was to purify and strengthen him.

For many years, I had been buffeted by physical ailments. I knew that was a sickness from the devil but permitted by

God. To tell you the truth, that was the time I learnt to lean on His shoulders. Sickness, in fact, turned the other way round. I was basking in the warm sunshine of God's love and His presence. It turned out to be a compulsory rest in a sick bed. The sick bed, so to say, had become an altar of praise.

"He cuts off every branch in me that bears no fruit, while every branch that does bear fruit he prunes so that it will be even more fruitful."

[John 15:2]

The true followers of Christ have to take up their cross and follow Him who called us to this great ministry. There may be divine reasons why sickness afflicts God's chosen ones. We walk along the paths of sorrow and come across hardships. The effectual prayers of such righteous people are answered when they pray for others. Physical affliction is common to us all. Prophet "Elisha was suffering from the illness from which he died."

[II Kings 13:14]

The one who suffered from illness and died was able to bring back a dead man alive! The miracles of Elisha continued even after his death! Physical ailment may be the cause for the death of a prophet. However, the spirit of the prophet in his dry bones is not dead.

"One while some Israelites were burying a man, suddenly they saw a band of raiders; so they threw the man's body into Elisha's tomb; when the body touched Elisha's bones, the man came to life and stood up on his feet."

[II Kings 13:21]

A similar thought is echoed in Ezekiel's vision of the valley of dry bones. When he prophesied, breath entered them. They came to life and stood up on their feet – in a vast army.

Some of the tombs of the saints of our nation must be well maintained; we may see such miracles taking place in our days too. God will heed to the prayers of his believers if they assure to work in His vineyard, because:

"The harvest truly is plenteous but the labourers are few."

[Matthew 9:37]

Many pray for the longevity of life only to covet somebody's wealth in their remaining years and to continue to lust after fleeting carnal pleasures. The prayers of such men are not answered since they hunt after worldly fame. They are of no use in His vineyard. God with His marvellous wisdom takes them to his abode. The great vision of eternity of life will be lost in such believes if they are allowed to live longer. It is stated about Daniel that he was sick for some days. St. Paul's thorn remains a mystery. Some Biblical scholars suggest that it must be a physical ailment. His follower Timothy was suffering from a weak constitution and therefore St. Paul, his spiritual guardian advises him to take wine. Speaking about Epaphroditus, Paul makes this statement:

"For indeed he was sick nigh unto death; but God had mercy on him."

[Philippians 2:27]

In the case of Joseph and Job, we could not trace the reason for their pain. They led a blameless and worthy life. Yet they were thrown into the fiery trial, which was to try their faith. Job takes up the rightful heir-ship and pours out his heart to our Heavenly Father. The whole Book of Job is the heart's cry of a man of sorrows. He presents his woes before the throne of the God of Justice.

"I would order my cause before Him; and fill my mouth with arguments."

[Job 23:24]

The greater the pain, then mightier are the gifts of compensation, and they are given in abundance. One, who had seen more hardships in life, is able to reach the broken hearts with divine compassion.

When I stand as a living testimony before people and share the love of God, they are easily touched. I do not talk of His love when things are going on smoothly without impediment. I speak of His loving kindness in the midst of sorrows, after I met with the tragic calamity of the death of my husband. Every verse in the Bible is 'yes' and 'Amen'. It is true in my case when I read the following verse:

"A bruised reed he will not break, and a smouldering wick he will not snuff out."

[Matthew 12:20]

The state of my being in those days was like David and his men who felt their life as the most miserable one.

"David and the people that were with him lifted up their voice and wept, until they had not more power to weep."

[I Samuel 30:4]

The wick in my lamp was about to be snuffed out when the storms from various ways were attacking me. I was like a little lamp floating on the waters of an ocean. The storm was raging outside to destroy the lamp. I lost my last hope in life. All around me was darkness, despair and disillusionment. Satan came with great wrath to steal my Jesus and make me deny His name. The wick in my lamp was about to be snuffed out. I was facing the storm, face to face and I sent the words directly to him with authority.

"How was thou not afraid to stretch forth thine hand to destroy the Lord's anointed?"

[II Samuel 1:14]

The Lord's anointed belongs to the Lord. And no one can destroy the Lord's anointed. The real living miracle is the way God collected all broken smithereens and reassembled them together to keep as a testimony for His glory. He lighted my lamp and dispelled darkness from me. I rejoiced with King David.

"You, O Lord keep my lamp burning; my God turns my darkness into light."

[Psalm 18:28]

"No pain is sent without a purpose." This sentence was given to me by the Holy Spirit on one of my special occasions. Once, I had to prepare a message for a select audience. I was

particular to give a right word to the gathering. Therefore, I waited at the Lord's feet for hours. It was a dramatic experience. I came swirling all along on a wooden plank in a jubilant spirit and with a dancing step. I made a sudden leap higher and was about to fall. I thought I was jumping into a swimming pool. However, to my great surprise, I was thrown into a very big merry-go-round chair. It started to move slowly. I saw my own shadow on the ground – all the time I was clapping my hands in joy like a little girl. All of a sudden, I was thrown to the sky. I could feel the pull of somebody who accompanied me while holding my hands. I stopped at a place. I knew not where I was. But I heard a very majestic voice saying this to someone:

"No pain is sent without a purpose; it is confidential."

The next minute, I was back in my room.

I realized that I could not ask the reason for the suffering I endured. Certain mysteries remain secrets. God my father knows what is good for his daughter. Therefore, I yielded myself with a total submission to His will. Peace began to reign supreme in my heart. I know it well that my times are in His hands and all things work for good. Does pain remain a mystery? Yes. Because the mystery of our Lord is surrounded by clouds. *"There came a cloud overshadowing them."* (Mark 9:7)

"He was taken up and a cloud carried Him up from their view."

[Acts 1:9]

Even St. Paul, with his penetrating gaze, could only say that he saw 'through a glass darkly'. We know Jesus by reading the four Gospels. Though they are the inspired books, they are not magical books, and we see Him in them veiled as in a cloud. Our own experience tries to pierce the cloud of mystery and thereby we know Him through the visions of saints but their visions are not our own. Each one comes to know Christ only through a cloud.

All of us have to go to the throne of God only through such clouds of unravelled mysteries. Perhaps, this discipline of perplexity best trains our character and shapes our soul. Again, another reason may be that we have a share in our Lord's passion of suffering. Unless we enter into the cloud of His pain, we cannot really enter into the light of His love. When our beloved brothers go through such a darkened cloudy atmosphere that presses upon them, we can share with them our gleams of light, shoulder their burdens and give them words of cheer and encouragement. If joy has come into our life, let us think that God was there first; therefore that joy is to be turned into thanksgiving. In a similar vein, if we experience some great sorrowful moments, some bitter pain, God is there first; God knows all about it. He is watching us with concern that we should not be defeated by our sorrow; instead, He wishes that we should gain spiritual education from that experience. God, who has worn a crown of thorns, knows our sorrows and He can make it beautiful.

At times, we feel perplexed at God's ways. Though we may not understand His ways, we can trust them because God is holy and will not do anything contrary to His character. *"Your sorrow shall be turned into joy."* (John 14:20)

A woman in labour pain knows her hour has come. When her baby is born, she laughs over her pain with joy and forgets it. Now she knows that the baby she gave birth to has come through her pain. The agony Christ went through had been the travail pangs of the passion; this is the loveliness of the love of God.

In winning a soul for His Kingdom, we may go through difficult times, but only through those difficulties, a good man will be born. Out of the travail that comes from self-surrender and self-discipline, a righteous man shall be born. One who earns the soul for Christ goes almost nearer to death through birth pangs. Therefore, pain in life serves as a prelude to a fuller life.

The Lord by His Holy Spirit gathers unto Himself those who have made a covenant by sacrifice. He is looking for those who will sacrifice themselves for Him and His service. Our Lord has come into His garden – the company of believers to gather myrrh and spices, the acts of sacrificial service in the cause of righteousness. Our Lord has promised to return and therefore on that Second Coming Day He will gather us unto Himself. Let us make a jubilant shout, and say, "Even so, come, Lord Jesus."

Lilies stand for purity, though they are often found among thorns. The plan of God for the church is that she should develop in purity and perfection. She is a consecrated flower, set apart for God's service.

Jesus puts forth a question in Matthew 6:28: *"Consider the lilies, how do they grow?"* They are perfect when they break the ground. They are perfect when they begin to bloom. It is a delightful sight to see all the silken clusters, chaste and white as they bloom. Passers-by do not see the thorns, the sharp piercing needles that may cause pain. Instead, they see the lilies, the pure and beautiful ones. The company of believers-the church-has to live among all kinds of people, yet must be separated. Jesus ate and drank with publicans and sinners, but He never became like any one of them. Instead, His presence sanctified the company. The Holy Spirit who dwells in the heart of believers can transform the wicked into new creations.

The fragrant smell of lilies of the valley attracts the attention of the passers-by even from a distance. When the seal of an alabaster jar is broken, the room is filled with fragrance. Similarly, there comes a sweet smell from a lily blossom that lives in the midst of thorns. What adds purity, beauty and fragrance to a lily is its background of thorns.

Where there is love there is the spirit of endurance to suffer. Our Lord courted the Cross for the sake of the love He had for us. Suffering is passion and passion is suffering. Hence, His chosen bride embraces pain willingly for the sake of her Bridegroom to bring forth more babes to Him.

Part II

Why does my Lord delay his coming?

Preface to Part II

The greatest event in future will be the coming of our Lord, Jesus Christ with power and glory. We have the authenticated Scripture verses that tell us of the advent as a personal manifestation of Christ once again, visible to all human eyes. His Coming will be sudden and unexpected as that of a thief in the midnight and ready to quell the rebellion that was started by Satan and his devils.

Christ indeed arrived once, but the epochal Second Coming of the Lord belongs to the future.

He came as a babe born in a humble manger in Bethlehem, and was finally abandoned and forsaken by all, to be crucified on the cross. However, in the crucial moment of His second coming, He will come *"in His own glory and the glory of His father and the holy angels."* (Luke 9:22-26) *"He will come as King of Kings and Lord of Lords, victorious over every foe."* (Rev. 12:5)

Two thousand years ago, He came as the Son of Man. He told His disciples in all humility that the Son of Man came not to be ministered unto, but to minister others. But when He comes again, 'every knee should bow Him'. (Philippians 2:10)

Habakkuk the prophet saw violent arguments and acts of violence everywhere. The violence involved strife and contentious quarrel among people. He cried out, *"O Lord, how long shall I cry, and thou will not hear! Even cry out unto thee of violence and thou will not save!"* (Habakkuk 1:1-2) God makes him understand that He is in control of all events. A vision of the end time was given to him. When God's people read it, they need to run and proclaim the news to the world. As times goes on, the message will become more important and urgent. God reveals to us more about the coming destruction, which is at the doorstep.

"And the Lord answered me, and said, write the vision and make it plain upon tablets that he may that readeth it. For the vision is yet for an appointed time, but at the end it shall speak, and not lie; though it tarry, wait for it; it will surely come, it will not tarry."

[Habakkuk 2: 2-3]

The prophecy of Habakkuk contains a message, for God tells us that there is 'no more delay' in end time events, culminating in the dramatic return of Jesus Christ. However, it is a warning to certain groups, sects, cults and theorists who deceive the weak and the innocent by their deceptive philosophy. God is calling them to repentance. The Lord's delay in coming is due to such rebellious and stiff-necked scoffers. Those who work sincerely in His vineyard may undergo the toughest trials but it is for a greater purpose. No pain is sent without a purpose. Enduring pain will bring a reward at the end.

Jesus Christ will return at the appointed time and it will be a new day for the whole of humanity to celebrate.

The Author

Why Does my Lord Delay His Coming?

The coming of Jesus

Is there a Second Coming? Will it take place? The Son of God who foretold of His arrival has not turned up for a very long period of two thousand years. All those who proclaim His Gospel sincerely are feeling weary and tired because of the delay in His arrival. "Behold, I come quickly" – the Son of God, who said these words to John, His beloved disciple, is coming very soon to take back His chosen ones according to the covenant He has made.

Now, why is there such a long delay in the promise He has made? All prophecies stated in the Scripture regarding His birth, life, death and resurrection are fulfilled except His Second Coming. The delay in His coming back in all glory with his angels has thrown many into a kind of complacent attitude. They have even stopped waiting for that great occasion; they have turned their attention to fulfil their personal needs – pleasure seeking, craving for everything that is in the world and the lust of their eyes. They also boast of what they have done. We should all remember the time has come. He has already forewarned us through John in the Book of Revelation:

"He that is unjust, let him be unjust still; and he which is filthy, let him be filthy still; and he that is righteous, let him be righteous still; and he that is holy, let him be holy still; And behold, I am coming soon! My reward is with me, and I will give to everyone according to what he has done."

[Revelation 22:11, 12]

Hence, the genuine workers of His vineyard are eagerly looking at the sky every day when they wake up from bed in the dawn and before they go to sleep. The repeated phrase uttered during the whole day in the midst of their work is:

"And the Spirit and the bride say, "Come!" And let him that heareth say, "Come!"

[Revelation 22:17]

Still He has not yet come. God gave this revelation of his Son's Second Coming to His servant John, which in turn must be shown to all His servants about things that will shortly happen.

The oft-mentioned prophecy in the Book of Revelation is:

"For the time is at hand."

It rings like a refrain of a ballad, almost ringing mildly into the ears of the listeners. The musical tone bears gentleness and at the same time, there is a majestic splendour as it reminds people incessantly to be ready for the grand ceremony – the Day of the Lamb to be united with His bride.

Consider other prophecies that are spoken in the Scripture. Are they fulfilled? Do those prophecies stand valid before the eyes of the people? To what extent have such prophecies stood the test of time and proven true? About the birth of this Son of God, Jesus Christ, it was revealed to the prophet Isaiah.

"Behold, a virgin shall conceive, and bear a son, and shall call his His name Immanuel."

[Isaiah 7:14]

The prophecy continues:

"For unto us a child is born, unto us a son is given, and the government will be on His shoulders. And He will be called Wonderful counsellor, Mighty God, Everlasting Father, Prince of Peace."

[Isaiah 9:6]

The end of that suffering-servant is spoken by Isaiah the prophet, in the following manner:

"He hath no form, nor comeliness"; and when we see him, there is no beauty that we should desire him. He was despised and rejected of men; a man of sorrows, and acquainted with grief; Like one from whom men hide their faces; he was despised, and we esteemed him not.

Surely He hath borne our grieves and carried our sorrows; yet we did esteem Him stricken smitten of God and afflicted.

However, He was wounded for our transgressions; He was bruised for our iniquities; the chastisement of our peace was upon Him; and with His stripes, we are healed…

He was oppressed, and He was afflicted, yet He opened not His mouth; He is brought as a lamb to the slaughter, and as a sheep before her shearers is silent, so He openeth not His mouth…

He hath poured out his soul unto death; and He was numbered with the transgressor; and He bore the sin of many and made intercession for the transgressors."

[Isaiah 53: 3, 4, 5, 7, 12]

To fulfil these prophecies of historical events there comes a grand scene of dramatic significance with the story of the all-powerful and mighty Son of God, our Lord and Saviour Jesus Christ. A Virgin, by name Mary conceived in her a babe that is of the Holy Spirit. Her child was called Jesus, for he was chosen to save His people from their sins. "Now all this was done, that it might be fulfilled which was spoken of the Lord by the prophet saying, "Behold, a virgin shall be with a child, and shall bring forth a son," and they shall call His name Em-man-u-el, which being interpreted is, "God with us." [Matthew 1: 23]

The dramatic scene shifts now to the temple in Nazareth, where He had been brought up; He went into the synagogue on the Sabbath day as was His custom and stood up to read.

There was delivered unto Him the book of the prophet Esa-ias. When He had opened the book, He found the place where it was written:

"The Spirit of the Lord is upon me, because he hath anointed me to preach the gospel to the poor; He hath sent Me to heal the broken hearted, to preach deliverance to the captives and recovery of sight for the blind, to set at liberty them that are bruised…"

Then He closed the book, gave it again to the minister, and sat down. In addition, the eyes of all that were in the synagogue were on Him. And he began to say unto them, "This day is this scripture fulfilled in your ears."

[Luke 4: 16-21]

Another new scene unfolds at Golgotha, the place of skulls. Exactly as the prophetic saying of the Old Testament speaks of crucifixion, here do we see Him being crucified between transgressors and interceding for them to His heavenly Father. Again, the prophecy about the division of His garment was also fulfilled. *"This happened that the scripture might be fulfilled which said, they divided My garments among them and cast lost for My clothing."*

[John 19:24]

Was there any note of His resurrection mentioned anywhere? As we turn the leaves of the last chapter of the Book of Luke, we come across these verses:

"And they found the stone rolled away from the sepulchre, but when they entered, they did not find the body of the Lord Jesus."

Two men in shining garments told them, *"He is not here; but is risen! Remember how he spake unto you when he was yet in Galilee? The Son of Man must be delivered into the hands of sinful men, and be crucified and on the third day rise again."*

"Then they remembered His words."

[Luke. 24: 2-8]

Promise of Power from on High

Our Saviour's command to the Apostles is:

"Tarry ye in the city, until ye be endued (clothed) with power from on high." [Luke 24:29]

It is an experience so definite that one could know whether he had received it or not. The same thing is clear from Paul's very definite question to the disciples at Ephesus.

"Did ye receive the Holy Ghost when ye believed?"

[Acts 19:2]

Paul evidently expected a definite 'Yes' or a definite 'No' for an answer. There should not be vagueness or indefiniteness in our answer. One may be regenerated by the Holy Spirit and yet not be baptised with the Holy Spirit. The disciples at the last supper were found regenerated but not baptized with the Holy Spirit. To be regenerated by the Holy Spirit is entirely different from the baptism with the Holy Spirit. When Jesus says, *"Ye are clean, but not all,"* he means that there was one unregenerated man, Judas Iscariot, who was not clean. Regeneration does not bring completion in a man, but the Holy Spirit, the comforter, does. This comforter can come only when Jesus goes back to prepare mansions for us. This is stated concisely in Acts 1:8, *"Ye shall receive power after that the Holy Ghost is come upon you; and ye shall be witnesses."*

When a man is baptized with the Holy Spirit there will be new power, a power not his own, but 'the power of the Highest'!

The baptism with the Holy Spirit is the coming of the Spirit of God upon a believer; He takes possession of all the faculties of a believer imparting to him gifts not naturally his own. The Spirit of the Lord qualifies him for the service to which God has called him. The timid Peter becomes a bold rock, remains unshaken in his faith, and proclaims the word of God in a thunderous voice. Every word of Peter goes touching people's stony hearts with power and conviction. Very strangely, he, who spoke against suffering, wrote one full chapter on suffering, suffering for the sake of Christ!

Baptism with the Holy Spirit is a necessity, Jesus said. Jesus charged them not to depart from Jerusalem, but to wait for the promise of the Father:

"For John indeed baptized with water: but ye shall be baptized with the Holy Ghost not many days hence."

He has strictly charged his followers, not to take up that great mission that was entrusted to them without receiving power from above. This power is necessary for their work, he said. His followers who had taken training under their Master for three full years did not start their work. They knew well that they had to proclaim Christ's teachings to the world. Mere preparation or training was not enough to go out and work. He instructed them 'not until then' – they should begin their work after they were baptized with the Holy Spirit. God anointed Jesus of Nazareth with the Holy Ghost and with power so that he went about doing good and healing all those that were oppressed by the devil.

To do God's service effectively, the baptism with the Holy Spirit is essential. Any Christian who is doing God's service without this baptism should stop his service and should wait patiently at the Lord's feet until he is 'clothed with power from on high'.

The followers of Jesus waited patiently, singing and praising God to receive the power. They were waiting in obedience to their Lord's command. Did they lose anything when they left the world and its affairs for Christ's sake? No. By preaching the word of God, they came out shining victoriously and shook the nations.

Many believe that the experience of baptism by the Holy Spirit is meant for the apostolic age alone. No. The Bible is the definitive book, which gives a definite answer that this possession of power is to be inherited by all, in all ages. Otherwise, there would not be a verse like this in the book of Joel:

"I will pour out My spirit on all people. Your sons and daughters will prophesy; your old men will dream dreams, your young men will see visions."

[Joel 2:28]

The same prophecy is quoted by Peter on the day of Pentecost. He said that it had been fulfilled when the Holy Spirit came on Jesus' disciples. Paul mentions that God would pour down His spirit upon Jews and non-Jews without distinction. When Peter addressed the crowd, people were cut to the heart as his words came out with power and conviction. They asked Peter and the other apostles, *"Brother, what shall we do?"*

Peter replied, *"Repent and be baptized, every one of you, in the name of Jesus Christ for the forgiveness of your sins. And you will receive the gift of the Holy Spirit. The promise is for you and your children and for all who are far off-for all whom the Lord our God will call."*

[Acts 2: 37-39]

Here Peter distinctly asserts that the gift of the Holy Ghost, 'the promise' – is for all believers in all generations. According to the word of God, this promise of power is given to men of all ages. Now we are living in an age of the Holy Spirit who is keeping His dominion over us all.

We have now come to a place where there is a deep sense of fulfilment of the prophecies of the Old Testament. A mysterious figure, a Messiah, emerged as the prophet foretold. He was a suffering Servant and through his suffering on the Cross, he provided a way to redeem the entire world. His suffering was of immense value to all the Jews who were scattered.

They are also chosen to undergo the experience of the baptism of the Holy Spirit. Times of suffering have tested and refined the true people of God. What next? The Son of God has to appear on the clouds in all glory with the retinue of angels, and blasting the sound of trumpets.

A Flash Backward

The angels who proclaimed the birth of Jesus to Virgin Mary, Joseph and the shepherds, and the angels who told of His resurrection to Mary Magdalene and other women, also spoke of His Second Coming to His disciples.

"After He said, He was taken up before their very eyes, and a cloud hid Him from their sight."

They were looking intently up into the sky as He was going, when suddenly two men dressed in white stood beside them.

"Men of Galilee," they said, "Why do you stand here looking into the sky?"

"This same Jesus, who has been taken from you into heaven, will come back in the same way you have seen Him go into heaven."

[Acts 1: 9-11]

Jesus Himself, like the angels, spoke of His Second Coming. The Book of John ends with a moving scene in which Jesus asks Peter,

"Simon son of John, do you truly love Me?"

This was a painful reminder to Peter of his denial of the Lord before the people. Then Peter is reinstated into the Great Commission of preaching the gospel to nations. When Peter saw John following him, he asked,

"Lord, What about him?"

Jesus answered, *"If I want him to remain alive, until I return, what is that to you? You must follow me."*

[John 21:22]

We note His words, which were casually thrown to the listening ears, *"Until I return."* It sounds as if someone were to go out somewhere for some time and then come back soon. The followers of Jesus, ever since then, have been eagerly waiting for His return. The believers are seen actively involving themselves in the Great Commission, and waiting for His return.

The last supper Jesus had with His beloved disciples is a more touching scene in the Book of John. Each one is moved to tears as Jesus began to speak of His going back to His Father. They listened to his moving talk with tears welling up in their eyes. Those eleven fearful men did not comprehend what He meant by 'going away' and sending a 'comforter' to them. He meant he was leaving the earth to return to His Father. However, the spirit of the Lord would come and reside in their body.

"I will not leave you as orphans; I will come to you."

[John 14:18]

"I am going away and I am coming back to you."

[John 14:28]

"In a little while, you will see Me no more, and then after a little while you will see Me. Now is your time of grief, but I will see you again and you will rejoice, and no one will take away your joy."

[John 16:22]

All the words of Jesus are fulfilled one by one except His physical manifestation. The scholars of theology use the term 'Epiphanies', which means manifestation.

The Day of the Lord will be a glorious celebration in heaven and on earth. It is likened to a grand wedding feast of the only son of God, the Bridegroom, and the redeemed soul of his bride. Preparations are being made on all sides – the heavenly procession of the Bridegroom with angels and the chosen bride here on earth.

"When the Son of Man comes in His glory, and all the angels with Him, He will sit on His throne in heavenly glory."

[Matthew 25:31]

The coming of the Lord is spoken of by Paul, when he visited Thessalonica, at one of the crucial moments of distress he faced from all corners. He was longingly waiting for the moment of rapture.

"We are left till the coming of the Lord... For the Lord Himself will come down from heaven, with a loud command, with the voice of the archangel and with the trumpet Call of God... After that, we who are still alive and are left will be caught up together with them in the clouds to meet the Lord in the air."

"For whenever you eat this bread and drink this cup, you proclaim the Lord's death until He comes."

[I Corinthians 11:26]

Daniel was given a series of visions. God showed him the pattern of future history. He foresaw nations rising in battle against nations and people suffering for no fault of theirs. They are left in such a sad state until God Himself comes to rescue them from all their troubles. He foresaw people falling down and worshipping:

"One who was like a Son of Man."

"In my vision at night I looked, and there before me was one like a Son of Man, coming with the clouds of heaven."

"He approached the Ancient of Days and he was led into His presence. He was given authority, glory, and sovereign power; all peoples, nations, and men of every language worshipped Him. His dominion is an everlasting dominion that will not pass away, and His kingdom is one that will never be destroyed."

[Daniel 7: 13-14]

Zephaniah, like other prophets, talks repeatedly about 'the day of the Lord'. There was hope offered to a humble remnant if they would seek God.

"On that day the Lord's sacrifice on that day I will punish…The great day of the Lord is near – near and coming quickly."

[Zephaniah 1:8, 14]

Listen! The cry on the day of the Lord will be bitter.

Still some sects, who hold a new cult theory, are of the opinion that Jesus is not in heaven; therefore, there is no truth in the forecast of His Second Coming or of His Judgment. These men are instructed to read the story of Stephen as how he was thrown to death for the bold statement he made about the vision to the Sanhedrin.

"When they heard this, they were furious and gnashed their teeth at him. However, Stephen, full of the Holy Spirit, looked up to heaven and saw the glory of God, and Jesus standing at the right hand of God. "Look," he said, I see heaven open and the Son of Man standing at the right hand of God."

[Acts 7: 54, 56]

They stoned him to death. His death with a prayer of forgiveness to the persecutors was a great testimony to young Saul.

A Flash Forward

Jesus Christ was probably returning to Bethany, and there He sat down by the wayside to take rest. The Mount of Olives stood directly facing the temple, from where He could have a full view of the temple. He sat there as a Judge upon the bench and thus he passed sentence upon the temple and the city.

The disciples began to ask him:

"When shall these things be? And what shall be the sign of the coming? And of the end of the world?"

[Matthew 24:3]

They were utterly perplexed by the predictions He made. At the same time, they were eager to know about the future events. Christ, in his answer, looks further than their questions and instructs his church concerning the great events to come, the destruction of Jerusalem, and His Second Coming at the end of time. He told His disciples to prepare themselves for the great event that would surely happen. Meantime, they must not be deceived by false doctrine. Seducers are more dangerous enemies to the church than persecutors. During this discourse, three times, He mentions of the appearance of false prophets and He warns them not to be ensnared by their doctrines. They, who killed true prophets and the true Messiah, will be easily ensnared by false prophets and Messiahs. The appearance of this kind of allurement towards false doctrine will be a true sign for the arrival of the Lord Jesus Christ.

These false prophets and false Christs will be busily engaged in drawing innocent people to their fold. They would even appoint more agents and sub agents to do this. When troubles begin to threaten on all sides, people will look for deliverance. Anything that looks like deliverance will be easily accepted by the people. They would cry saying "Lo here! Lo there!" People should not allow themselves to be deceived. Christ is overall, and He will not be seen here or there. He will come in all His glory to collect them on a particular day. That day will be a momentous one in history.

These false Christs, Christ said, would come forth with great signs and wonders. If His people happen to see signs or wonders, they must not follow them because they would allure His people to serve other gods. These are the lying wonders wrought by Satan, the prince of the power of the air. Satan does it thus to deceive his people because he has already obtained permission to do so. We must remember the magicians of Egypt who by their arts of divination and enchantment performed signs and wonders not for the glory of God but themselves. Christ wished His select ones to protect them from any kind of delusion. Our saviour gives repeated warnings to His disciples advising them to stand upon their faith through the word of God. The greater enemy to true faith is credulity; the simple believe every sign and wonder, and run after every cry.

'Beware of believing' is our motto. Every pretender will come forth with a new gospel. We must not go after people who say, *"He is in the desert" or "He is in the secret chambers."* Let us not be carried about with every wind. Man's curiosity to know new doctrine will land him in a fatal apostasy. However, sitting still and waiting at our Sovereign Lord's feet will give us strength.

Another sign will be the great commotion caused by wars. Nations shall rise up against nations. We shall ever hear of wars and rumours of wars. The chosen ones of God need not be troubled by such news. The heart that is fixed, trusting in God and his mighty power will enjoy peace, which will flow like a stream. All these wars have to take place because the justice of God must be established. The honour of the Redeemer who laid down His life on the Cross for the redemption of His people must be asserted.

All these things must happen because every situation is governed by our Sovereign Lord. Evil is allowed to move but only to meet its own end. Even then, the end is not yet, for worse things will follow. An affliction of one type will be but the beginning of another. God's chosen ones are expected to fight against the devil with a steadfast mind, willpower, and determination. They have to pull up all courage and encounter what is set before them.

Our Lord says, "Be not troubled to hear of wars and rumours of wars; for then what will become of you when the famines and pestilences come?"

"And if we be frightened at a little brook in our way, what shall we do in the swellings of Jordan? If running with the footmen weary us, how shall we contend with horses?"

[Jeremiah 12:5]

He foretells other judgments, which will be sent by God soon after war. They are famines, pestilences and earthquakes. Once when David was asked to choose one of these punishments for his people, he was at a loss. Everything was dreadful and painful. Likewise, famine and pestilence and the consequences of every war will be terrible.

Then He tells us of the persecution that would happen to His own people; some of them will be tortured and put to death. This will dilute the faith of many and there will be decay and deterioration in religious doctrine thereupon. Blood of the saints will run like water on the streets. They will die several times a day in the hands of tyrants. They shall undergo cruel mocking and scourging. They will not be killed at one stroke; but they will be tortured and killed slowly all day long.

The world will rise against them; they shall be hated by all nations for Christ's sake. Among the believers, there will be many misunderstandings. Many will begin to fight among themselves. The great faith will be put to question. They will grow weary and tired in following Christ and his doctrine. They are the weathercocks. They will follow Christ when the weather is fine to them. When they face storm, they will immediately quit the place and run.

When the power mongers execute punishment, the believers will begin to betray one another. It will be a pitiable sight to see them diffused with envy, enmity and malice. The wolves in sheep's clothing will wander about everywhere and will begin to show their original colour, by throwing off the wolf's clothing. Treachery and hatred will be seen everywhere. Love will not be seen anywhere. One brother shall deliver up another brother to death. Love of many shall wax cold.

Elijah felt that he was the only one left alone, a true man of God with his steadfast faith and so he cried unto the Lord for his safety. However, the Lord comforted him saying that he was not the only one. There were men living, His remnant, whose knees had not bowed down to Baal or to other gods. They still live with a zeal for God's glory. In a similar vein, love that remains cold will not be dead; but will shoot up with new tender leaves when spring comes. Of hope, the English poet Shelley writes:

"If winter comes, can spring be far behind?"

Winter should be followed by other seasons. Likewise, God's chosen remnant will stand with integrity of mind and steadfast zeal for the glory of God, even in the worst of times. Some of them will endure such persecution to their very end. These people will stand in support of the Lord's message. They will seek their refuge under His Cross.

"He that endures to the end shall be saved."

Those who persist in unbelief shall be damned.

Before the end, the gospel of the Kingdom of God shall be preached everywhere. There will be greatest opposition to the preaching of the word of God. However, the word with all its power will make its way through the times of trouble and persecution. Some may fall by sword or flame; yet the gospel shall be preached. Some may accept Jesus as their saviour. When the gospel is preached everywhere, 'then shall the end come'. Throughout His discourse, He was saying, "Not yet, not yet." At the end, He says of the ruin that was coming upon the Jews, their city, temple and nation.

Christ's Second Coming is here foretold in this way.

There will be the glorious appearance of our Lord Jesus. He will show Himself, as the Brightness of His Father's glory and the very image of His person, will darken the sun and the moon, just as a candle is darkened in the beams of the noonday sun. Then all the tribes of the earth shall mourn. All sinners will be mourners. However, the believers, who have sown in tears, shall shortly reap in joy. The impenitent sinners will look at Him whom they have pierced.

They shall see the Son of man coming in the clouds of heaven with power and great glory. That day will be the Day of Judgment. It is given to the hands of Jesus Christ. Christ went before Israel in the wilderness in a cloud. Now, the cloud is His judgment throne. His first coming began with all humility in a humble manger; but His Second Coming will be with power and glory.

He shall send His angels, who will go forth with a great sound of trumpet. They are His angels, because he is the Son of God. Moreover, they wait upon Him to carry out His order. Trumpets will be sounded to call people and gather them into one fold. The sound of the trumpet will be terrible and alarming, which will wake up people from their long stupor. The elect of God seen scattered from one end of heaven to the other end shall be gathered by angels.

"However, as to that day and exact hour of the arrival is hidden from the eyes of all people. It will be sudden as the floods that came and destroyed the land during Noah's time. People Knew not until the flood came, and took them all away; so shall also the coming of the Son of man is."

[Matthew 24:39]

There is a certain day and hour fixed for the Judgment to come; it is called the Day of the Lord. That day and the hour are kept secret. No man knows it; even the wisest of men does not know it. However, many leaders of cult theories fix a date of our Lord's Coming, as they wish, and deceive a larger group of innocent people. Some were led to suicidal attempts too. As we all know, the suicidal wish is not from God, but from the devil, who is busily engaged in enlarging his kingdom in hell. Perhaps the delay is due to such false prophets. Jesus has clearly stated:

"None knows but my Father only."

People in Noah's time were not aware of the destruction that was near their doorstep. Drinking or eating is required for one's mere survival. Drinking and eating alone is not life. They were following the epicurean philosophy of life: "Eat, drink and be merry." Instead of repenting and praying, they were seen indulging in sensual pleasures. They were careless because they were secure in their homes. They neglected Noah's warning.

"They knew not until the flood came."

Similarly, people today will not know until they see the Day of the Lord. People want to indulge in sensual pleasures because they live in secure homes. All are in deep slumber like those five foolish virgins. When the bridegroom arrived, they did not have oil in their lamps. In modern times, everyone is off his watch and at his ease, comfort and luxury. We see churches today growing in large numbers and congregations growing larger in number. Sabbath day service is followed by a feast of God's plenty in every dish! Jesus wished to feed the people because he was filled with compassion. They did not have food for three days. They may faint on the way, he thought. Therefore, He fed them, blessing them with five loaves of bread. Today's churchgoer is a follower of the epicurean philosophy. Perhaps, the delay is due to this!

People in Noah's time were in their own world of self-indulgence. Modern man is still in his deep slumber. The terrible blasting trumpet of the angel will be sounded to awaken the sleeping world. We do not know where the sleepy Virgins and lovers of sensual pleasures will run and hide themselves on the Day of His wrath. Those who mocked at Him and about His coming will be taken away by the wrath of the Lamb.

Second Coming Day will also be called a Separating Day; if two are at work in the field together and one of them is a believer, he will be taken into a place of shelter and the other will be left to the sword of the enemy. Between two women at grinding work, one who belongs to Christ will be offered safety and the other will be abandoned.

In all these examples, the urgency to accept Christ as their saviour is repeatedly stressed, to escape from the day of wrath. The prophet Zephaniah says:

"Thus the meek of the earth are hid in the day of the Lord's anger."

[Zephaniah 2:3]

His elect people are seen intermixed with others in the same habitations and employment areas. A true Christian will neither be abandoned nor forsaken by God. God knows how to separate the precious from the common, the gold and dross from the fiery furnace, and wheat and chaff in the same threshing floor.

Meantime, the one and only duty expected of a true Christian is to 'watch and be ready'. There is a delay in the arrival of the Lord because we are still in slumber and are not ready to receive the bridegroom. We are asked by our master to be awake and keep ourselves awake. Sleeping is an inactive state; but watching and praying is a gracious and wakeful state. At this end time, God's grace is abundantly poured in great measure upon all of us. The Spirit and the bride say, *"Come!"* But the flesh is not ready to co-operate with the spirit. We are instructed by our Master to be diligent and keep vigil always. When we are ready with our lamps, trimmed well with a bright burning wick, we shall not wake in vain. We shall have, then, our bridegroom to attend upon and prepare ourselves to do things that will please the Lord.

A master of the house will guard his house against any peril that may cause ruin to his house. The children of this world are wise. When they know of a danger approaching, they will keep awake and stand on their guard to protect their house. That house is our own souls. We must be ever alert and attentive. By praising and waiting at the feet of the Lord, our spirit will keep aflame, burning with zeal.

His parting word was, *"Surely I come quickly."* This parting word obliges us to live in a state of expectancy. He has also stated that,

"I come quickly, In such an hour as you think not."

The Day of the Lord comes by surprise as a thief in the night. The bridegroom came when the virgins were in slumber. A true Christian is expected to observe Esther-fasting and Deborah-vigil to receive the Lord. Are we true to our Lord's expectation? Perhaps the delay is due to this!

Through Parables

The Lord's coming will be a happy one to all His faithful servants; but the same day will be a dismal one to those unfaithful servants. Christ comes to render reward or punishment to every man according to his work. A wise steward's sincerity and humility will be recognized by the Master when he returns to settle the account. He shall be called 'the Blessed' by the Master. Thus, Christ on that great day will confer honour and glory on all those faithful servants.

The wicked one does not believe in Christ's Second Coming. He says in his heart:

"The Lord delays His Coming. He will never come. He has completely forsaken his church." Thus he begins to doubt the Lord's coming, and hence his heart is hardened to do evil. He is a steward appointed by the Lord to look upon the servants of his household as his own fellow servants. This way he can show humility to his neighbours. But he is seen smiting his fellow servants, which is not pleasing in the eyes of the Master. Moreover, he smites his fellow men under the assumed authority of his Master. This is detestable in the eyes of the Lord. Again, this evil steward is seen associating with drunkards.

"He begins to eat and drink with the drunken."

He has developed intimate fellowship with them. He loves such evil company. He has the gifts of learning and is talented in uttering a message above others. It is of no use since he is seen indulging in wickedness. Doom is waiting for him about which he remains insensitive. Hell is the place reserved for such hypocrites.

Christ delays His coming because He wants to be kind towards such indifferent people; He wants them to be saved and brought to His fold. His delay talks of His gracious nature and patience. But wicked people, whose hearts are hardened because of their wicked ways, begin to doubt His arrival.

The Israelites, God's chosen ones, in the absence of Moses began to make an idol – a calf made of gold – and fell down in prostration before it in the form of worship. This was abominable and repulsive before the eyes of the Lord. His eyes are pure, and he cannot tolerate evil. He comes down to judge people. It grieves the heart of the Father to see that His own elect ones are going after idols and start worshipping them. Perhaps the delay is due to such evil stewards who lead an ungodly life.

Let us escape from His wrath, because 'death and damnation' are reserved for wicked servants. They will be thrown to the place of everlasting misery, where there is nothing but 'weeping and gnashing of teeth'. They trample down the holy blood of Jesus. Their profane and immoral lives are ever before His eyes. Those who preach to others must put their preaching into practice.

He who is now our Saviour in this grace time will be the Judge at the end times. Zephaniah, like other prophets condemns the sins of his nation and goes further by predicting the judgment of God. He is the one to talk about the Day of the Lord.

"The great Day of the Lord is near and coming quickly."

"Before the fierce anger of the Lord comes upon you, before the day of the Lord's wrath comes upon you..."

"Be silent before the Sovereign Lord for the day of the Lord is near. On the day of the Lord's... On that day, I will punish."

[Zephaniah 1:14, 2:2, 3 1:7, 8, 9]

Jesus concludes His discourse with the parable of the Ten Virgins. He urges us all to get ready for His Second Coming. The parable of the three servants warns us to prepare ourselves carefully and be ready to settle our account with Him. There is a tone of urgency in His discourse.

The Song of Solomon and the whole of the New Testament portray Jesus Christ as the Bridegroom. The redeemed souls of men by His holy blood are the chosen brides of Jesus. There is a delay in His coming because the bride is in deep slumber. There is no excitement in His arrival for her – not even joy. The preparation for the Bridegroom's return has already started. The Bridegroom, who has prepared such a glorious procession in heaven, is much grieved at the complacent attitude of His bride. She has not arrayed herself in ceremonial robes like a queen for that grand occasion. She does not even show anxiety. It was for her and for whose sins the Lamb was slaughtered; it was for her and for whose scarlet garments to be washed, He shed His holy blood to the last drop on the cross. He laid down His life on the cross as a sacrifice, so that His beloved may live a peaceful life, freed from her guilty conscience. He thought that His bride would long for His arrival, day in and day out. However, to His great surprise she is seen living a carefree life in secure homes. She is lukewarm – neither warm nor cold. The Spirit says, "Come Lord Quickly" with a passionate heart. The Spirit in her is willing to get ready and prepare herself to meet the Lord. However, the flesh is weak. The disciples at Gethsemane were not able to keep themselves awake an hour in prayer when their saviour was about to be handed over to the Roman soldiers. It grieves the Holy Spirit to see His chosen ones in deep slumber without any excitement of His Second Coming. Perhaps the delay is due to this complacent attitude of the bride!

Believers are now betrothed to Christ; but the solemnizing of the marriage is reserved for the great day, when the bride, the Lamb's wife, will have made herself completely ready. In the Book of Revelation, those who follow the Lamb are called virgins. The word 'Virgins' denotes purity and beauty. St. Paul is of the same opinion when he says, *"They are to be presented as chaste Virgins to Christ."* (II Corinthians 11:2)

As Christians, we should not only profess our love but also love and long for the coming of Christ. We long to praise and exalt His name. However, we never praise Him whole-heartedly. We profess ourselves the attendants upon Christ to do Him honour. To do Him honour and service, we need the lights in our hands. We are the light of this world, as we follow the One who said:

"I am the way, the truth and the life; and I am the light."

One who received this light will not keep it under a bushel but keep it on the top so that people will walk in the light.

A true Christian will spread radiance around him. His cheerful countenance is like a bright candle lighted in a dark room. The gospel we carry in our hands is the light we carry to the world. We carry good news to the world. We comfort, encourage and cheer up the depressed souls. Sincere Christians are the wise virgins and the insincere are the foolish virgins who took their lamps but no oil. It is an outward show that they are getting ready to meet the Lord. Their mere show and pretension will be seen in due course, by the whole world. They act under the influence of external inducements, but are void of spiritual insight.

Their hearts lack the knowledge of sound doctrine. Therefore, they are labelled as hypocrites. The place assigned for hypocrites is hell. Hence, let us surrender our showy nature to God and plead with him to remould us. Thereafter, we can work with sincerity for His glory.

The wise virgins took oil in their vessels along with their lamps. They also supposed that the Bridegroom might tarry. They had a good principle; they had love for the Bridegroom and above all, they had faith in Him. Our light must shine before men for a longer period. The oil refers to 'grace' that we have in our hearts. This oil keeps the lamps burning.

What was the common fault during the Bridegroom's delay? They all slumbered and slept. First, they slumbered and then they slept. The Bridegroom did visit. He did not come to the spot as they expected. Christ may tarry past our time, but He will not tarry past the due time. He has not accomplished many things. He comes back to gather a good harvest; but to gather a good harvest the earth and heaven must be made ready. The elect of the earth are to be collected and the saints of heaven are to be tried.

The wise virgins kept their lamps burning, but did not keep themselves awake. What does it show? They love the Bridegroom; yet they have lost their first love – love that had its zeal, passion, liveliness and grace.

I am coming soon. Hold on to what you have, so that no one will take your crown…

"Yes I hold this against you; you have forsaken your first love."

[Revelation 3:11, 2:4]

There was a cry made. The bridegroom arrived. They heard a call that whipped them saying, *"Go ye forth to meet Him."*

They all arose and trimmed their lamps. The lamps of the foolish virgins were gone out. The saying goes, *"The candle of the wicked snuffed out." "Give us your oil,"* the hypocrites made an earnest appeal to the wise. The wise could not spare. What they all had was very little for them to stand before God. They could only answer thus: "Lest there be not enough for us and you; Go ye rather to them that sell."

They went out to buy; that was not the time for buying and selling. The shops were closed. While they went out to buy, the Bridegroom came. He came in pomp and splendour, dressed in rich attire as the King of Kings and Lord of Lords, accompanied by His friends. They that were ready went in with Him to partake in the marriage of the Lamb. There they had God's plenty to enjoy.

When the Bridegroom's party stepped in, the door was shut. This was like the shutting of the door of the ark when Noah and his family went in. Those who get admittance into the celestial city are secure, enjoying eternity. There will be an everlasting feast where the bride will be brought in and the

"Bridegroom will rejoice over His bride."

[Isaiah 42:5]

The abandoned are the ones who missed the grace time. When the foolish virgins came back, it was too late. They cried out, *"Lord, Lord,"* but they were rejected. However they pleaded and demanded for entrance, yet they were shut out. Their vain confidence could not get them their admittance. They received only the reply:

"Verily I say unto you, I know you not."

The parable concludes with our beloved master's warning:

"Watch therefore..."

The kingdom of heaven is likened to a man travelling into a far country, who entrusted his work to three servants. When Christ ascended on high, he was like a master who was travelling into a far country. Each one was given talents to work with.

Each began to work with God-given gifts and graces. They traded with their talents and were successful. God's stewards must have something to show about their sincere work to their Master. The Master expects the talents to be multiplied. When the Master came back and asked for the account, the first two servants showed forth their work and the profit they received. Their labour of love was well rewarded with the titles conferred on them, 'good and faithful servant'.

The third one makes the confession stating that he buried his talent in the earth. The excuse he gives is more ridiculous, "You are a hard man – and I was afraid." With all audacity, the servant says. *"I knew thee to be so."*

Our God is not a God who demands bricks without supplying straw. Indeed he arose to anger, when he saw the injustice done to His people by the Egyptian Pharaoh who, without supplying straw, demanded bricks to be made.

His grace is immense. The immediate verdict comes out from the judge:

"Thou wicked and slothful servant – you are sentenced to be cast into outer darkness."

A slothful servant is an unprofitable servant to any master. Many are given talents to work effectively for His service. Some are like this lazy servant who would never do anything good for Christ. Probably the delay of His Second Coming is due to such slothful servants – who simply sit doing nothing!

Jesus will come back when we least expect His arrival. The only way a servant can remain true to God is to be ready for the Lord's surprise visit. We must wait for our Lord with great expectancy in our hearts, just as a little girl waits for her Dad's return from work, with all faith. She does not have any doubt in her father's return. On seeing her father at the corner of the street, she will be the first one to step out, run, and receive him. The Lord expects this childlike faith from each one of us.

Do we see Jesus in our clouds? He said, *"Behold, He is coming with clouds..."*

[Revelation 1:7]

Clouds are the sorrows and suffering we endure in our lives. Yet it is through these very clouds that the Spirit of God is teaching us how to walk by faith. *"The clouds are the dust of His feet."* (Nahum 1:3). They are the sure signs that God is there. We see Jesus face to face only in the midst of our sorrows, and during the hour of bereavement. God cannot come near us without clouds. He wants us to unlearn something. He wants to teach us something in our trials. How many of us are thankful for the trials we face in our lives? Are we not like those Israelites who wandered for forty years in wilderness, always grumbling and murmuring? We knew it well that 'our times are in His hands' and 'All things worketh for good'. Knowing it well, many grumble. Perhaps the delay is due to those grumblers who never budge an inch to praise God and exalt His name!

The Judgement of the Day

The description of the process of the Last Judgment on that great day of His Coming is given in detail in the Book of Matthew. Son of Man takes His judgment seat. This judgment brings everlasting happiness to His believers and misery to those who did not accept Him. The Judgment of the great day is entrusted to the hands of the Son of Man, by His Father. Once again, His arrival is stated as the most glorious and splendid one by the apostle Matthew:

"When the Son of Man shall come in His glory, and all the holy angels with Him, then shall He sit upon the throne of His glory."

[Matthew 25:31]

The whole world shall see the brightness of His Father's glory. He shall come not only in the glory of His Father, but also in His own glory. This glorious Lord will come with a retinue of holy angels who will wait on Him.

So long He was seated on the throne of mercy interceding for us all, to the Father. Now, at His Second Coming, He will sit as a judge in the court of law. All men and women on earth, from all occupations, will be gathered. So long the wicked and the god fearing were living in all parts of the world together; but on the great day, they will be distinguished one from another just as the good fish are separated from the bad ones at the sea shore, and as the corn from chaff in the threshing floor.

The god fearing is the sheep to stand at the right side of the throne. No sinner can hide himself and run away from the group of sinners; no one saint will be left among the sinners. The separation will be exact because the Judge is a good shepherd who knows His sheep.

The godly are like sheep – innocent, mild, patient and useful. The wicked are like goats, which are known for their base nature – rebellious, obstinate, callous and unruly. The godly will receive the pronouncement as 'blessed' and the wicked as 'cursed'.

God has made us heirs of heaven. We come to an inheritance by virtue of our son ship—if children, then heirs. The godly are ever happy because they know their son ship, which was purchased by His holy blood.

What do the prophets speak of the End Times?

Jude's warning note comes as a loud-sounding alarm. The tone of Jude is stern and hard-hitting.

"See, the Lord is coming with thousands upon thousands of His holy ones to judge everyone, and to convict all the ungodly for all their ungodly acts they have done in the ungodly way, and for all the harsh words ungodly sinners have spoken against Him." Jude asks the believers to be patient and persevere in the midst of grumblers and faultfinders.

"In the last times there will be scoffers who will follow their own ungodly desires... Keep yourselves in God's love as you wait for the mercy of our Lord Jesus Christ to bring you to eternal life."

[Jude 1: 14, 21]

Every vision a prophet speaks of becomes reality. A prophet is a chosen vessel of God to speak of God's will. The prophets mentioned in the Old Testament uttered predictions of things to come. Their work is only a small part in God's great plan. When a prophet speaks, he speaks for God, carrying messages of truth and duty, of faith and hope for the present, interpreting the events of the present and predicting things to happen in the future. Such prophetic predictions are seen in the writings of all prophets like Isaiah, Jeremiah, Ezekiel, Daniel, Micah,

Nahum, Habakkuk, Zephaniah, Zechariah and others. God spoke to the prophets of the Old Testament in dreams and visions. Their very language is veiled with symbols and images. It uses figures of speech.

Their prophecies speak of victory over the serpent under the figure of his head being bruised. Isaiah speaks of his overthrow by picturing him as having dust for food and John, the beloved disciple of Jesus, portrays him as one bound in chains. All the prophecies of the Old Testament prophets were fulfilled to the letter at Christ's first coming.

In the New Testament, Jesus Christ talks of the end of the world. He had many more things to share with His disciples. However, they would not be able to comprehend what He said, He thought. *"I have yet many things to say unto you, but ye cannot bear them now."*

All the prophets prophesied in an ecstasy. Their state was a supernatural one. Paul was giving his messages out of his own experience. He was certain that he was caught up to the third heaven; but he was not able to tell if he was in the body or out of the body. In the language of the prophets, we come across phrases like:

"I was in the spirit and heard"; "The hand of the Lord was upon me"; "The Spirit of the Lord came upon me."

Peter saw a vision, but he did not know whether it was in ecstasy or trance. First, he took the literal meaning of the vision he saw: of unclean birds and animals creeping, which were inside a large sheet. Later, he understood the spiritual significance of the vision. The whole Gospel age is looked upon as the end-time or, "It is the last time." There is not the least doubt in the fact that with the ascension of Christ and the descent of the Holy Spirit, the last period of the world's history had begun. The believers have already become the citizens of heaven. The believers are mystically united to Him and therefore they are with Him in a spiritual sense, inhabiting the eternal world. Every believer belongs to the heavenly world but lives in the earthly sphere. He is a heaven dweller; he is here on earth to mortify all the organs of his body. He belongs to Christ. His soul will enter into the heavenly homeland at death; on the great day of the event of Christ's coming, his body as well as his soul, will inherit the eternal order. Therefore, a born-again Christian longs to be forever with the Lord in heaven. He longs for His coming; to his chosen ones the day of the Lord is connected with judgment. Various Bible interpretations are given about the return of the Lord.

What is meant by Greek word 'Parousia'?

The Greek word 'Parousia' means personal presence and is used to mean the return of the Lord, as that event relates blessings to the godly and destruction to the ungodly. The Greek word 'Apokalupsis' means 'unveiling' or 'revelation'. This word makes an assertion of the visibility of the Lord's return. The scholars hold different views regarding His return. The theologians distinguish between 'the rapture' and the 'revelation'. There takes place 'rapture' at Christ's sudden and secret coming in the air to snatch away His chosen ones, and 'the revelation' takes place after a seven-year interval of trouble following 'the rapture'. They say that the first event – the rapture or day of Christ, will have no signs to mark its approach, while the second event, the revelation or day of the Lord, will have the signs of His approach. All these terms, *'The Day of the Lord'* [I Thessalonians 5:2], the *'Day of Lord Jesus'* [I Corinthians 5:5], *'Day of God'* [II Peter 3:12], *'That Day'* [II Thessalonians 1:10], and *'Last Day'* [John 12:48] refer to the great epochal event at the end of the world. One thing is certain. When Christ comes, He comes to bless and reward His people and to judge the world in righteousness.

Divine Wrath on that Day

Divine wrath is confined to the Day of the Lord. When the wrath comes, it only touches the wicked. The passages in the Bible speak of the wrath falling on all men, rich and poor, strong and weak, and on the kings of the earth and commanders. Everything is recorded to show that God is just while passing His judgment upon people. The divine wrath is waiting for the arrival of the Day of the Lord. The Church is promised exemption from the divine wrath.

"I will keep you from the hour of testing. There will be genuine preservation and protection of the church during the hour of testing."

[I Corinthians 15:11]

The fate of the earth on that great day is described by Peter. The present time, in which we are now living, will be destroyed by fire.

"But the day of the Lord will come like a thief. The heavens will disappear with a roar, the elements will be destroyed by fire, and the earth and everything in it will be laid bare."

[II Peter 3:8]

"The Lord knows how to rescue godly men from trials and to hold the unrighteous for the day of judgments."

[II Peter 2:9]

St. Paul is of the opinion that when the coming of the Lord takes place, there will be a jubilant noise among believers. He talks of the rapture of believers on that great day.

"For the Lord himself will come down from heaven, with a loud command, with the voice of the archangel and with the trumpet call of God, and the dead in Christ will rise first. After that, we who are still alive and are left will be caught up together with them in the clouds to meet the Lord in the air."

[I Thessalonians 4:16, 17]

But the same day will be a day of distress to all unbelievers.

"God is just; He will pay back trouble to those who trouble you…

This will happen when the Lord is revealed from heaven in blazing fire with His powerful angels… They will be punished with everlasting destruction and shut out from the presence of the Lord… on the day He comes to be glorified in His holy people and to be marvelled at among all those who have believed."

[II Thessalonians 1:6, 8, 9]

The coming of the Lord is not a mere story, invented by disciples, says Peter:

"We did not follow cleverly invented stories when we told you about the power and coming of our Lord Jesus Christ, but we were eye witnesses of His majesty."

[II Peter 1:16]

Moreover, Peter warns his brethren saying:

"The Lord is not slow in keeping His promise, as some understand slowness. He is patient with you, not wanting anyone to perish, but everyone to come to repentance."

[II Peter 3:9]

Therefore, the central message is that everyone should repent and receive this great gift of redemption. The Second Coming is postponed for you and me. His slowness in coming back reveals that He is patient and gracious. He is a God of compassion. He does not want to punish people unnecessarily. Jonah speaks of God's nature when He did not destroy the city of Nineveh.

"I knew that you are a gracious and compassionate God, slow to anger and abounding in love, a God who relents from sending calamity."

[Jonah 4:2]

Love of Money is a Sin

Paul addresses Timothy that believers should flee from all kinds of temptations especially from the temptation of love of money. *"For the love of money is a root of all kinds of evil."*

[I Timothy 6:10]

"He charges them to keep this command without sport or blame until the appearing of our Lord Jesus Christ."

[I Timothy 6:14]

People today who want to become rich overnight fall easily into the trap of foolish and harmful desires set by Satan. Usury is the root of all social evil. Believers of Jesus Christ are seen with this evil practice of lending money at a high rate of interest. A usurer is a usurper, who wrongfully takes somebody's power, authority, position and property.

"Some people eager for money have wandered from the faith and pierced themselves with many grieve."

[I Timothy 6:10]

It is high time for believers to check their attitude towards money. Money earned through dishonest means had already taught us the lesson of a bitter end that was met by Judas. Blood money earned by crushing the innocent, enabled the Pharisees to buy only a blood land, out of those 30 pieces of silver. Many have changed God's ministry. His name is not exalted but blasphemed among non-Christians. We know very well what had happened when Jesus Christ came with a whip lashing at the moneylenders, who were lending money and selling things in the House of God. Let us wait for His arrival with a clean hand.

St. Paul advises Titus and his fellow brothers to live a self-controlled, upright and godly life until 'the glorious appearing of our great God and Saviour'.

[Titus 2:13]

Evangelists, who were mightily used by God, have fallen into the miry pit of disgrace because of their love of money.

His advice to Titus was to rebuke the Cretans sharply for they are 'always liars, evil brutes, and lazy gluttons'. This is an important factor we Christians, have to unlearn – lying, brutal acts and gluttony combined with laziness. The Lord delays His coming because we have not yet given up some of our strong attachments that grieve the spirit of the Lord.

Two thousand years ago, *"Christ was sacrificed once to take away the sins of all people; and He will appear a second time not to bear sin, but to bring salvation to those who are waiting for Him."*

[Hebrews 9:28]

Surrender of that something that has special meaning for your soul and spirit

The soul of a man is bound to the things of this world. This grieves the Lord. Jesus said, *"This kind never comes out except by prayer and fasting."* (Matthew 17:21) Fasting does not mean the mere giving up of food for the body. It can mean surrender of something that has a special meaning for the soul and spirit. Giving up certain attachments can be more difficult than physical fasting. We love to cling to our own idols —idol like money, property, ego, the feeling of superior race, the sense of belonging to a high caste; our attachment to these things dilutes our prayers. They are not fervent and earnest. God can hear and answer the prayers of those who give up their ego – the feeling of 'I'. Until we throw away our ego and cling only to the Lord, the Holy Spirit will be teaching us lessons so that we shall be sanctified. During fasting, one should consider where his soul is attached. Some of us may feel – *"Oh, I hope the day never comes when God will ask this of me."* What we in secret are attached to must be surrendered whole-heartedly. When one gives up that to which he or she is attached, then God begins to perform miracles. God listens to the prayer of the righteous. The prayer of the righteous has incredible power because it is now earnest, heartfelt and continued. Above all, the soul is freed from bondage. God expects to surrender to Him, which means a release from all bondages. He likes to hear the cry of the humble and loves to answer the prayers of the repentant hearts and thereby take all glory to Himself. An adverse circumstance in life helps us to show to the Lord that one's hope is in Him and Him alone. What idols are there in us, to which we cling with deeper attachment? The delay is due to such idol worshippers. Let us not grieve the Holy Spirit who is in us.

Mockery is a Sin

Jesus Christ speaks of His Second Coming to his disciples in Matthew, chapter 15; in the next chapter, He speaks of it to his enemies to terrorize them. Nothing is more comfortable to the righteous, or more terrible to the ungodly, than Christ's judging of the world on the last day.

"Thou tell us whether thou be the Christ, the Son of God? Jesus saith unto him: Hereafter shall ye see the Son of man sitting on the right hand of power, and coming in the clouds of heaven."

[Matthew 26: 63, 64]

The High priest rent his clothes saying:

"He hath spoken blasphemy."

Then they banged Him, and some smote him with the palms of their hands. They made sport of Him, as the Philistines did with Samson. As a mark of abuse, 'they spat in his face'. Thus, the Scripture was fulfilled. He did not hide his face from shame and spitting. Job makes the same complaint: *"They spare not to spit in my face."* (Job 30:10) People usually spit on the ground. The face of Jesus was thus treated as the ground; the face, which was fairer than the face of children, the face, which was white and ruddy, the face, which was adored by angels with reverence, was now abused by the basest and vilest of men. Spitting on one's face is an expression of contempt and indignation.

They made sport of him in all possible ways. People were growing merrier and merrier when they saw Him in a state of misery. Again, as an additional reproach, He was crucified in the midst of two male criminals, as if He were the principal criminal. To complete the humiliation of the Lord, the common people that passed by reviled at Him. The Book of Matthew records all the taunts and jeers of the common people who uttered words of mockery:

"Save thyself."

"If thou be the son of God come down from the Cross, and we will believe."

"He saved others; Himself He cannot save."

[Matthew 27: 40, 42]

We do come across such mockers in our day-to-day life everywhere. Paul had already forewarned about such godless people who will ridicule the god-fearing in the last days.

"There will be terrible times in the last days.

People will be lovers of themselves…

Boastful, proud, abusive…"

[II Timothy 3:1]

"Yet these men speak abusively against whatever they do not understand."

"…these he has kept in darkness, bound with everlasting chains for judgment on the great day."

[Jude 1:10]

"Whoever corrects a mocker invites insult; whoever rebukes a wicked man incurs abuse."

"Do not rebuke a mocker for he will hate you"

[Proverbs 9: 7, 8]

"A mocker resents correction"

[Proverbs 18:12]

It is 'of no use to rebuke scoffers'. They are incorrigible. Such scorners are arrogant disdainers of others. They are classified as fools by Solomon. The prophet Habakkuk speaks of a scorner:

"See he is puffed up; his desires are not upright… he is arrogant and never at rest".

[Habakkuk 2: 4, 5]

The Spirit of the Lord is grieved at the attitude of the scorners. This is high time for the mockers to change their attitude. The delay of the Lord's coming is due to such scorners.

The righteous are called the blessed of His Father and the wicked are asked to depart from Him. To be near Christ will give solace, comfort, satisfaction and joy. The very presence of Jesus will give us peace that passes beyond human understanding. However, to depart from Him is the hell of hell. It brings destruction when one is away from the presence of the Lord and from the glory of His power. The ungodly are sent to an everlasting fire. Those who served Christ are taken to be with Him and those who served the devil when they lived on earth are sent to be with Satan and his companions in the eternal fire.

Being uncharitable to the poor is a damning sin:

"The doom of the uncharitable will be dreadful. They were like epicureans living at ease and luxury; they were not grieved for the affliction of Joseph."

[Amos 6:5]

They were merciless towards the poor:

"Blessed are the merciful, for they will be shown mercy."

[Matthew 5:7]

The Moabites were excluded from going to the sacred altar because they

"…met you not with bread and water."

[Deuteronomy 23:3]

The doom of the persecutors will be cruel on that day. Those who slighted and persecuted poor Christians had actually slighted and persecuted Christ Himself. What was done against the faithful followers of Christ, the Judge on that Day takes it as a great offence done against Him.

When the Lord was hungry and thirsty, they gave Him neither food nor drink to quench His thirst. He was treated as a stranger and was banished from their company. When He was in distress, they were selfish, and busy with their own comfort and pleasure. They were reluctant to part with their money; their money could have been spent usefully to establish the kingdom of God. The righteous on the other hand, shall inherit the kingdom of God. The beloved soul will be united with the Bridegroom.

Occult Practice

What grieves the heart of the Lord is the practice of occult, seen among nominal Christians. His own people stand and burn incense before manmade idols. St. Paul had already made a prophetic warning: *"Now the spirit speaketh expressly, that in the later times some shall depart from the faith, giving heed to seducing spirits and doctrines of devils; speaking lies in hypocrisy; having their conscience scarred with a hot iron."*

[I Timothy 4: 1-2]

The situation today is becoming graver. Books on occult are selling in great numbers. In many conventional bookshops, books on the occult have completely taken over one long shelf that was once reserved for other books.

What is abominable unto the Lord is expressly given in the Book of Deuteronomy:

"There shall not be found among you any one maketh his son or his daughter to pass through the fire; or that useth divination, or an observer of times, or an enchanter or a witch or a charmer or a consulter with familiar spirit (medium) or a necromancer."

[Deuteronomy 18: 10-12]

His divine wrath is graciously postponed for such lost sheep. Satanism or devil worship can no more allure people, for the whole earth is going to be filled with God's grace in the end times. People should give up occult practice; otherwise, they will be abandoned on Judgment Day. It is worthwhile to remind ourselves of the warning note of John the Baptist – *"Flee from the wrath to come."*

Deceptive Philosophy

We are living in the last days – and the predicted apostasy is already here. It is preparing many for their doom. It is turning away men from their faith. Faith is the faith once delivered to the saints. We have to contend earnestly for the faith that was once for all entrusted to the saints – God's people.

"Let no one deceive you in any way…"

[II Thessalonians 2:3]

False doctrines have swept the believers of the church in this evil hour. Churches have succumbed to the seduction of such false doctrines as binding demons and loosing demons, positive confession, hyper-faith, inner healing methodology and methodology for healing of the memories and other therapeutic theories. People who dance and skip during worship time are at the heights of the Himalayas and at the next minute of their practical life, they fall headlong into a valley, throwing all their professed principles to winds. Churches are in a chaotic condition today. We are looking for a balanced assembly where there will be worship and spirit-filled messages of the word of God. They teach sound doctrine so that the spirit of the Lord can move without restriction, reaching people with conviction and power. We are eagerly looking for a church which is spiritually alive. The electrified atmosphere, which is genuinely filled with the presence of the Holy Spirit, makes the demons flee and heals the sick.

Such fellowship is denied to Christians because ignorance abounds in churches. Some do not give sound, deep, Bible teaching and the congregation is alarmingly ignorant of the word of God. They do not even realize the need to study the word. Under the protective word of tradition, the congregation is in deep stupor, reciting stereotyped prayers composed one thousand years ago, which lack freshness and vitality for today's needs. Violation of tradition alone will bring out man's innate power to stand for Christ with zeal and determination. Shallow theories leave one in a puzzled state; they lack the determination and will power to take up the Cross daily and follow Christ.

"My people are destroyed from lack of knowledge. Because you have rejected knowledge, I also reject you as my priests."

[Hosea 4:6]

As we are in end times, let us not allow ourselves to be deceived by false doctrines. God hath graciously delayed His coming for those sheep that hath gone astray from the pen to return.

Stay in the city until you have been clothed with power from on high.

Many evangelists go out to preach the word of God with their mere salvation experience. They argue that the 'baptism with the Holy Spirit' was for the believers of the apostolic age alone. Their heads are crammed with knowledge and information. They try to explicate the verses of the Bible in their own way. They preach the truth, the truth as it is in the Gospel, in its simplicity and purity; but preach it 'in persuasive words of wisdom' and not 'in demonstration of the spirit and of power'. (I Corinthians 2:4)

They preach in the energy of the flesh and not in the power of the Holy Spirit. It is dangerous to preach the word of God without the power of the spirit. A man whose head is crammed with knowledge and information cannot give life to the listener. Life or Spiritual Death to a listener depends on whether we preach the Lord's word without or with the baptism of the Holy Spirit. Those who involve themselves in God's ministry must not be satisfied with their salvation experience alone. They can do our Lord's work effectively if they ask for the special anointing from above. The delay of our Lord's Coming is due to such people who are not clothed with the power sent from God.

Covetous Nature

God gave us Ten Commandments through Moses, His chosen vessel. One of the commandments is:

"You shall not covet your neighbour's house, neighbour's wife, or his man servant or maid servant, his ox or donkey, or anything that belongs to your neighbour."

[Exodus 20:17]

"Now if you obey me fully and keep my covenant, then out of all nations you will be my treasured possession."

[Exodus 19:5]

Habakkuk speaks of this covetous nature of his people in this way:

"Because he is as greedy as the grave and like death is never satisfied…"

"Woe to him who builds his realm by unjust gain."

"The stones of the wall will cry out, and the beams of the woodwork will echo it."

[Habakkuk 2:5, 9, 11]

Habakkuk finds his own people growing more and more violent. They are greedy and aggressive. The eyes of God are so pure that they cannot approve of this covetous and aggressive nature.

People today do not like to take 'No' for an answer to any of their problems. When they do not get what they want, they become angry and remain sulky. Somehow or other, they plot to exploit the innocent. It does not matter to them how they take or who gets hurt when they take. They ruin the joy of the blameless. They are filled with envious desires; they confiscate the belongings of the simple god-fearing people. The wicked commit more and more sins. Ample chances are given to them to repent. However, they never do so. Therefore, God's wrath is waiting for such men.

"What causes fights and quarrels among you? Don't they come from your desires that battle within you? You desire but do not have, so you kill. You covet but you cannot get what you want, so you quarrel and fight. You do not have because you do not ask God. When you ask, you do not receive, because you ask with wrong motives, that you may spend what you get on your pleasures."

[James 4: 1-3]

What actually destroys the unity among believers? Greed and evil desire corrode the church and destroy unity among believers. *"Instead, you ought to say, 'If it is the Lord's will, we will do this or that.'"*

[James 4:15]

Let us not boast or brag about. It is the right time for us to implore the Lord for forgiveness of our vile nature and escape from the wrath of God. Satan prepares many to face that Day— the Day of doom and damnation which is reserved for the ungodly. However, we Christians must prevail and pray. Let us wage a spiritual battle for such people and redeem them from the clutches of the devil.

The delay of our Lord's coming is due to covetous people whose desires are not upright.

Love Each Other

Jesus was having His last supper with His disciples. It was a touching scene when the Master was bidding farewell to His followers. It was Jesus' most anguished leave-taking ceremony. He gives a moving farewell address and an important last message to them. It was His commandment. Jesus said, *"It is for your good that I am going away."*

[John 16:7]

"A new Command I give you; Love one another. As I have loved you, so you must love one another. By this all men will know that you are my disciples, if you love one another."

[John 13: 34, 35]

We come across people who long for all spiritual gifts – gifts that should be gained in an unusual way in their ministry. However, the same people do not show a single fruit that comes out of love. Every man's faith is tested by the fruit he bears for Christ. These people cannot work for Christ in the midst of a larger group of men, with all inconveniences. They profess to live for Christ in the midst of the larger group of men, with all inconveniences. They profess to live for Christ but by their actions deny their faith. They lack love, joy, gentleness, self-control, patience, perseverance, tolerance, peace, kindness, goodness and faithfulness. We are asked by Christ to serve one another in love and to live a spirit-filled life. The believers ever live with a friction among themselves. Paul says, "Not I but Christ lives in me." Love of Christ must come and fill our hearts. A sect of people in church never step out of the church to purify themselves, saying that sanctification is more important than service. We can bring disciples to Christ only through love.

"My Command is this: Love each other as I have loved you," says Jesus Christ.

[John 15:12]

St. Paul speaks of love as the greatest one among faith, hope and love. A believer needs all gifts to do the Lord's ministry. Above all, simple love is superior to supernatural gifts. These spiritual gifts must be properly exercised in an orderly way without confusion. One may have the gift of prophecy and can fathom all mysteries and all knowledge. However, if he has not love he is only a resounding gong or a clanging cymbal. One may give all that he possesses to the poor and surrender his body to the flames, but if he has not love, he gains nothing.

The love of the disciples for one another is evidence of their love for Christ. Moreover, it is an ample proof of their gratitude to Christ. His Commandment is 'as I have loved you'. We should love one another because Christ loved us first. The new commandment is not to take revenge on people who do not love us but to show more of Christ's love to them. The old law was:

"Thou shalt love thy neighbour." Now the new commandment is, *"You shall love one another."*

Love and love alone must be shown to our brothers. The distinguishing character of his disciples is the way they loved each other. Every disciple of Jesus is noted for this brotherly love. They excel all others in loving one another.

The delay of our Lord's coming is due to such hard-hearted men whose hearts are filled with hatred, animosity and resentment. Our Sovereign Lord is a God of love and compassion and hence He expects His followers to show such love and compassion towards their fellow brethren. For example, a waiter in a restaurant before closing the bars of the door makes a plea: *"Hurry up, please! It is time."* Likewise, the Spirit of the Lord pleads the believers to change their lifestyle immediately, for we are living in the end times.

Purity Has Power

There is power in purity. Purity is power; it is the power of self-respect, the power of pleasing Jesus Christ. There is a distinctive life that helps one to avoid the scare of the scarlet sin, caused by adultery, and it grieves the heart of our loving Father, to see little babies that are born out of wedlock. A house that is built without marriage is like a house without a roof. God wants to see His people dwell in 'secure homes' and 'undisturbed places of rest'. Even great men meet with their downfall because of their folly of practicing impurity. A young man is expected to keep himself like Joseph, pure and flee from youthful lusts. Many evangelists had fallen because they were allured by a sinful world.

We come across many instance of young men who are brought up by godly parents, choosing a path of impurity.

They desecrate their body instead of consecrating it to God. They can very well implore forgiveness in this grace period.

God himself is the One responsible for our sexual desires. He created man and woman with drive for food, drink, sleep and sex. However, men and women choose of their own free will by selfishly giving place to unclean passions. Sex enjoyed outside marriage brings 'a wound and dishonour, a reproach that shall never be wiped away'.

When our loving Father gave us the Commandment, *"Thou shalt not commit adultery,"* it was for our benefit; because guilt leads one to a sense of isolation; anyone who sins, suffers and feels alienated. Very often, we encounter heart-breaking stories of men and women of Gospel ministry who sold their purity of 'a piece of bread' as the Book of Proverbs calls it.

"The prostitute reduces you to a loaf of bread… a man who commits adultery lacks judgment; whoever does so, destroys himself. Blows and disgrace are his lot, and his shame will never be wiped away."

[Proverbs 6: 26, 32, 33]

Any such sinner can implore forgiveness to our Lord of mercy who readily pardons him of his guilt by washing him and cleansing him by the blood of Jesus Christ. He is the Lord of compassion. The Lord will completely sanctify us in a way that we shall be of great service to God; He shall set us apart as sacred and holy. We shall not be disturbed by evil thoughts of provocations from the flesh. The plan of God for the Church is that it should develop in purity and perfection. It is a consecrated flower, set apart for God's service. The delay of our Lord's coming is due to certain wrong guides who still recklessly lead impure lives. Let us rededicate our lives to God as Paul declares in Corinthians:

"Since we have these promises, dear friends let us purify ourselves from everything that contaminates body and spirit, perfecting holiness out of reverence for God."

[II Corinthians 7:1]

"Yes, I am Coming Soon."

[Revelation 22:20]

The other day, my daughter-in-law was admitted in a hospital for the delivery of her second baby. Earlier, she had read Jackie Maize's book, 'Supernatural Childbirth' several times. In that book, Jackie and Terry Maize share how a young mother can conquer labour pain and deliver the baby through the dynamic faith principle. My daughter-in-law's first one was a Caesarean and the second one, miraculously, turned out to be a normal delivery.

My grandson, a smart little boy of four, was waiting at the doorstep with great expectancy and excitement. They were strolling about in the ward for four long hours with love and trust.

It was strange to see the little boy when the elders requested him to go out and play. He preferred to stand and wait. His waiting at the doorstep with all eagerness for the arrival of the little baby was touching. Until the baby girl was brought out and shown to him by the nurse, he was waiting with hope and patience. The moment the door was opened and the nurse came out holding the girl baby in her arms, his joy knew no bounds. Pride and joy were seen sparkling and dancing in his eyes. Do we have this kind of excitement in our expectation of our Lord's coming?

With what eagerness do we wait for His Second Coming?

With what excitement and joy?

With what alertness and love?

Where there is love, there is expectancy.

There are two roads set before us. One is broad and the other is narrow. Thus, life and death, reward and punishment, good and evil, blessing and curse are set before us. The path we choose will decide our end. The upright and the chaste that hath not yielded to the lust of the eye and arrogance of the world will enter into His abode of joy. The lover and the beloved will reign supreme thereafter.

"This is what the Sovereign Lords says:

The days are near when every vision will be fulfilled… it shall be fulfilled without delay."

[Ezekiel 12:23]

People may ridicule that the vision a prophet sees is for many years from now and his prophecy is after all for the distant future. Hear what the sovereign Lord says: *"None of my words will be delayed any longer; whatever I say will be fulfilled."*

[Ezekiel 12:28]

The great epoch, which began two thousand years ago with the birth of Jesus Christ, is now ending. Cruelty and callousness prevail everywhere. Man has developed a callous nature, which he never had before. He has thrown away the cherished ideals of the past. Intellectuals who brag about their power innately lack moral conviction. They move with lack-lustre eyes because they have severed themselves from God and religion. Man has shed all the purity and innocence which once marked his actions. He has given up his faith in God, which was once a life-sustaining force in his life. Chaos reigns supreme everywhere. Therefore, the time is ripe for the promised Second Coming of Jesus Christ.

Part III

Set the Captives Free

Preface to Part III

The fruits of prayer I have enjoyed; now I want to share them with my readers. To bring them to this part, I committed it in the hands of God. He opened the doors for me and fulfilled this desire. Every step in writing this was guided by God and passed through prayer chains. While working as a prayer warrior, the methods I have explained here proved worthwhile in bringing several members and their families to join, kneel down and pray. When we followed these resources in group-study, I found the results exciting. Participants were thrilled to share their own experiences relating to the power of prayer. A prayer of relinquishment often brings desired results. They all accepted that praying in one accord and praying in God's will are always answered.

We discussed questions like – does God guide people today? Can we tune our ears to hear His voice? What are the hindrances to prayer? Can a prayer in a prayer-closet move people for whom we pray? Can that silent prayer change the stormy circumstances? Who is an effective intercessory Prayer Warrior?

Holding frequent Intercessory Prayer meetings brought blessings in the lives of people, I noticed. Most of them who attended those Bible Study hours were non-Christians. The Spirit of the Lord moved mightily when we arranged small open-air meetings in Indian villages. The way our Lord answered the requests of the villagers, little children in particular, was breathtaking.

Most people we see around us are bound by spiritual bondage. How are we to free them –and ourselves – from such bondage? There are three types of Spirits: the Holy Spirit of God, the Spirit of the devil and the human spirit. We fail miserably when we allow human intervention in taking our decisions. This is done out of our own anxiety to solve certain problems quickly. In spiritual warfare, God's intervention alone can bring victory. In one of my great moments of distress, I was thrown into despair – that was the time of bereavement when I lost my husband. I was not aware that I was under the control of 'self-pity', which was leading me on and on to a state of depression. I was made captive under its control for some time. However, by His immense grace, I was set free from the bondage. He gave me 'the garment of praise for the spirit of heaviness'. I desperately needed thoughts of hope to dismiss all negative thoughts of pessimism. The following verse gave me hope in life, and I found the purpose of my life.

"For I know the thoughts that I think toward you, says the Lord, thoughts of peace and not of evil, to give future and a hope."

[Jeremiah 29:11]

I found a great consolation when I realized that God has a wonderful plan for me; He plans to give me the expected end-plans to help me prosper and not to harm me. At times, I had to face a different struggle from outside sources. God's audible voice that strengthened me was: *"The battle is the Lord's;" "Trust in the Lord and don't despair."* Since then, I have learnt to wear the garment of praise. Praise is a powerful weapon, which released me from the bondage of despair.

It may seem that evil is winning gradually. But remember, Satan's days are numbered. He has already been defeated. Our Sovereign God puts Satan and his demonic hordes in their positions. When we realize this, we come to understand His power and enjoy our freedom. Satan knows that he and his followers will vanish before the very name of Christ. This faith gives us the fortitude to stand in the name of Jesus and claim our victory.

Who implanted a new heart and a new
spirit?

Losing one's own for ever

Leaving the other in gloom and pain.

Like a girl frightened and lost in deep woods…

Who knows not the way darkness engulfs.

Empty hands, which hugged children once

Stand far away in their hearts

As noon day cares, press them more.

Little children
With their prattling noise and giggle
May fill this empty room of mine I thought–
Faded is their love
As they are laden with mundane work,
Inconsolable on one side
Irredeemable on the other
Exhausted body with innumerable aches
Unutterable in the anguish of the mind,
How I longed to flee from this harsh world
A world that offers sad experiences
Broken is the heart in pieces
With untold sighs and groans
But this I know full well –
Assembling them in order
Is the work of the Great Master Artist.
I hurried to bang the Door of Heaven
Help came from the Spirit –
My sole companion here on earth.
Pat came the reply:
"No pain is sent without a purpose."

It's a voice majestic in utterance.

I felt it in my bones.

When I realized –

"Redemption is there at the cost of pain,"

My mind was filled with dizzy thoughts.

Is this the gift given to me?

To be desolate in despair

This then is the gift I give back to thee

A song of praise in pain may please thee more

A bleeding and bruised heart of mine

If that alone brings glory to His name

To Him I submit my entire being.

Me I submit, "A bruised reed,"

A smouldering wick"

I relive the past.

Closed he his eyes softly with a beam

Sank down his head with a tender whisper:

'Jesus', on his lips.

Just before the eyes of his devoted wife,

Just before the eyes of his beloved offspring.

What a glorious end

To end with a child-like trust in his Saviour.

I sit in the garage on a broken bench,

I see a vast desolate land before me.

The morning breeze is sighing around

Flowers arrayed in white

Look drooping

All due to yester night's downpour.

Wherein does lie security for His own?

I brood over…

Is He at work in me?

Is He at work with me?

Am I His workmanship?

Has the dawn He sent forth bear any message?

Out came a tiny painted butterfly

Somewhere from the cosmetic room

Of the one Great Artist

All clothed with glittering Starry powder

Brighter with varied hues of stripes and dots

Briskly landing on a flower

Jumping on to another with a rhythmic beat,

Simply glorious and marvellous to behold

It was a dancing girl's swift step,

All like a giggling thing of two –

Heaven sent angels to cheer me up!

His divine appointment –

Not an accident but an incident

He loves! He cares! He sustains!

At last –

A smile at the sight of "self-pity"

A demon fleeing from me

Freed once and for all – set me free

To zoom like a little dove in the air

It flutters its wings deep in my heart

His work is always the wonder

And His timing perfect

Deep in my being

His abiding Presence I feel.

Prayer: O Lord, heal all the broken-hearted,

As you healed me

In Jesus' name

I pray. Amen

The Author

Set the Captives Free

Stand Still and Know His Will

God's calling fist drives us to know what His Will is for us.

Instead of getting panicky about the situations that happen around an individual, he is asked to wait on God. Mary, the sister of Martha, chose the best in her life: the inseparable part she chose, by sitting at the Lord's feet. Martha, though she tried to please the Lord by her hospitality, was in fact, prone to irritation and a complaining nature. The mundane activities of the world disturbed her much more than the visit of Jesus or His gracious words. However, Mary's act of sitting at the Master's feet as an ardent disciple to learn had been highly commended by Jesus Christ.

Jesus loves such ardent disciples – disciples who would sacrifice their workday schedule for Him and wait on Him to hear what He speaks. The time may be forty days as Moses waited; as Jesus waited in the wilderness; as Esther waited for three days. He expects us also to wait on for more than two hours every day. He wants to share the hidden treasures of heaven with His chosen servants of God. He wants to bring a tremendous change in the spiritual growth of our life.

When the children of Israel saw the Egyptian army marching after them, they cried out to the Lord in fear. The vast Red Sea before them was the reason for their fear. In their fear they complained to Moses saying,

"...Because there were no graves in Egypt, have you taken us away to die in the wilderness?"

And Moses said to the people,

"Do not be afraid. Stand still and see the salvation of the Lord, which He will accomplish for you today."

[Exodus 14:12, 13]

The sea parted and the Israelites crossed through the path made in the sea. We see the salvation of individuals, our loved ones, the members of our family, or a nation, when we 'stand still'. Those who 'wait on the Lord' shall inherit the earth. He will accomplish everything for us.

The Lord loves His children who wait on Him. He will not allow them to wait more than a minute unnecessarily. For every believer, His presence is a safe refuge in the world. When we come under His care, He cares for our body, soul, mind and spirit. We should not hesitate to run to His presence. There may be many reasons tempting us to run away from His love. However, we should wait for His rescuing hand and His mighty power. Moses gains confidence to inspire the Israelites. We see his words of courage uttered with boldness:

"The Lord will fight for you, and you shall hold your peace."

[Exodus 14:14]

To wait on the Lord, one needs to have total trust in the Lord; he needs a solitary place to pray; he needs patience to wait until he gets the answer for his ardent prayer; he needs to offer prayer to His throne until one sees salvation for the souls he prayed for; and he should wait on the Lord. We have to wait for Him until we get the looked-for results; God need not wait for us. The period of waiting will be crucial for the intercessors.

No sooner had St. Paul heard of his call, than he went to the Arabian Desert and spent his time at the feet of the Lord. Only then, he came back to Damascus. Sadhu Sunder Singh in India, a great man of God, spent most of his time alone in the remote places of Tibet. All these men derived their inner strength only when they stood waiting for God and praying for long hours. This waiting on the Lord helped them in their ministry.

For any mortal waiting on the Lord is a painful experience, as he is to remain alone in solitary confines for days. When God chooses one to intercede for a multitude of souls, it is a painful experience. For, in the intercessory prayer session, God so gives His burden to the prayer warrior that he spends days together in lamentation. As a result, the intercessor first understands the call. Then he draws a plan to fulfil God's call. Having known his purpose in life, he decides to fulfil the desire of His heart. St. Paul for example, was given such a call. Immediately he rose up to know about the call with a determined mind.

Ananias told Saul:

"Brother Saul, receive your sight…"

Then he said, *"The God of our fathers has chosen you that you should know His will, and see the Just one, and hear the voice of His mouth."* (Acts 22:13, 14)

Paul wanted to know the will of God meant for him, and the will of God for the people he was meeting from that day onwards. Having known God's purpose in his life, he was baptized, and washed off his sins by calling on the name of the Lord. To find out the purpose, we are asked to wait at the feet of the Lord for some time. By knowing His will, we will work effectively in His ministry – some as evangelists, some as shepherds, some as prophets, and some as intercessory prayer warriors. In the midst of struggles, which we meet quite often, we read a Christian literature book, hear a verse read to us, get counsel from a man of God, but never decide to sit still and talk to God. We talk on and on about all things, but never wish to go on our knees and hold a talk with our Father. Reading is good; sitting in a Bible Study class is good; and finding useful principles from our reading is good. But we gain our inward strength through our meditation with the Lord. The victory is won when we realize the strength in us relates to our inward attitude. Hence, we realize that our strength does not lie in practising a principle or a technique, but in Jesus Christ our Saviour, at whose very name every knee will bow and every tongue confesses, *"He is Lord."*

By waiting at His feet, I confess that I do not rely on my own self-effort, will power, talent, my skill or my abilities. I trust Him alone, I say. For which I humble myself to the utmost and plead for His gracious hand to intervene in my moments of distress. I implore His grace to be present whenever I am led into terrible situations. I present my petition asking Him to grant me courage and confidence which He gifted to His servant Moses, when he was standing before the sea.

My intercessory prayer for whom I prayed was affecting them, I realized. An intercessor by remaining inside a room can change a situation or the entire world. He or she need not travel to meet people to bring changes in their lifestyles. However, in spirit, the intercessor can go to every country in this world.

Who is an Effective Intercessor?

When things go wrong, God expects someone to intercede for the wrongs of the people. God detests the abominations of the people and so His wrath is roused up to punish the people. But the prayer of an intercessor brushes it aside. An intercessor's role is an important one, which changes the history of a nation; sometimes it changes the decree of a country as in the case of Esther's intercessory prayer for the Jews. God wants interceding prayer warriors to plead for the cause of the people around them. In other words, these intercessors come closer to the heart of our Heavenly Father, sit at His feet for hours, months and years pleading Him to restrain His judgment hand on the wrongs of the people.

One of the great attributes of our Father is – His heart of compassion. Knowing this attribute of the Father, effective intercessors often point out His compassionate nature and get the degree of punishment lessened. The interceding prayers alone bring down His grace and mercy to people in lieu of His wrath and harsh judgment. Abraham, the father of faith, is a good example for intercessory prayer. He pleads for the defence of the city of Sodom, which was becoming known for its lewd behaviour. Their wickedness had almost reached a point when God could not withhold His hand of judgment any more.

Abraham's closer walk with God gives him courage to ask God question after question about His principles regarding judgment.

"Wilt thou also destroy the righteous with the wicked?"

[Genesis 18:23]

We must observe here the intercessory techniques Abraham adopts. He is steadfast in his mind to save the people from the oncoming judgment. He tries again and again, minimizing the number of fifty righteous men from fifty to ten. He is very polite while pleading for the people. God is equally polite while answering Abraham. It is something strange! An intercessor alone has the privilege to come closer to His heart. Hear the conversation that runs between man and God – almost like a conversation between two friends.

"Then he said, 'Let not the Lord be angry, and I will speak but once more: Suppose ten should be found there?' And He said, 'I will not destroy it for the sake of ten.'"

[Genesis 18:32]

God was compassionate to save Lot, Abraham's brother. We get a glimpse of the loving nature of God.

"...When God destroyed the cities of the plain, that God remembered Abraham, and sent Lot out of the midst of the overthrow, when He overthrew the cities in which Lot had dwelt."

[Genesis 19:29]

God remembered Abraham, the intercessor, and therefore saved Lot from being destroyed.

God's righteous nature does not tolerate people hurling abusive words against a man of God, especially an intercessor. On several occasions, Moses had stood at the gap pleading to God for those rebellious people.

He went to the extent of saying, *"Blot out my name from the book."* However, a congregation consisting of two hundred and fifty leaders rebelled against Moses and Aaron.

Their words of abuses were:

"They gathered together against Moses and Aaron, and said to them, 'You take too much upon yourselves, for the entire congregation is holy, every one of them and the Lord is among them. Why then do you exalt yourselves above the assembly of the Lord?'"

[Numbers 16:3]

"You have brought us... to kill in the wilderness that you should keep acting like a prince over us?"

[Numbers 16:13]

God's wrath came to consume them in a moment. However, Moses and Aaron fell on their faces and interceded for their men. They said,

"O God, the God of the spirits of all flesh, shall one man sin, and you be angry with all the congregation?"

[Numbers 16:22]

Again when people complained, God's wrath was about to consume them. Aaron, at the command of Moses, ran with incense burning, to appease the anger of God. So then, the plague that had started stopped gradually.

God did not allow even Miriam, the sister of Moses, to speak ill of Moses. She had to endure the affliction of leprosy for her ruthless words against Moses. All servants of God, including intercessors, are the chosen vessels of God. They are separated from the world for His work. They are set apart from the pleasures of the world. They are consecrated for His vineyard work. Already they have been led through numerous paths of agony and mental anguish. When people start to insult those intercessors who intervene for their cause, it grieves the heart of God. They do it in their ignorance. But truth is: God's anger is provoked even more because of this sin.

God has to judge the world because of the sins we have committed as individuals and as nations. Whenever we see our people violating God's law or hear their words of blasphemy – then we are to run to the gap and fill it up. The intercessors hold one another's hand and make a plea to heaven above asking for 'God's mercy – Christ's mercy'. We repeat the Lord's Prayer, "Lord, forgive us our sins!" As members of our own family, society, organization or a nation, we should implore forgiveness for their sins because we are accountable for the sins of other members.

We as a group had been in an Intercessory Prayer Session for 21 days, with prayer and fasting. We received numerous phone calls to pray for them. We all prayed in one accord to save those souls from the clutches of money, jewels and other pleasures of the world. We pleaded with an agreement in spirit to God, asking Him to check the powers of evil. People from outside, who joined in our prayer team, were cleansed of their sins. They gave their lives to God.

When we heard reports of demon-possessed women, we all prayed in one accord, pleading God to make everything new. Most of our prayers were for the lost souls. Our great wish was to set the captives of Satan free. We wished to hear signs of new life in the lives of prodigal sons and prodigal daughters. We silently gathered inside a small hall and shut ourselves the whole day; we fervently prayed for the hard-hearted nature of men and women to come to repentance. Within a short time, we saw results reaching us from far and near.

Vendors on the street preparing soft drinks use ice blocks. First, the ice blocks are put in jute bags, and the bags are beaten with handheld batons to make ice cubes. Once they get small ice cubes, they mix it in the soft drinks. The chillness added to the drink is delicious and palatable.

Before that, the ice was a hard huge block. To use it, it should be broken to pieces. We adopted this same method in our prayer session to break the hard-hearted nature of prodigal sons and daughters. Once they were kept under Satan's captivity. When the Holy Spirit was poured upon them, the very anointing broke their yoke. They were freed from all kinds of bondages. The Spirit of the Lord moved mightily in their midst; our prayer was done in a silent way – with sighs and tears; in hushed whispering tones we made prayer petitions to our God above. The results we saw were amazing.

Intercessors pray not for their loved ones or members of their family. This prayer goes in accordance with the heart-beat of Jesus Christ. Knowing His heartache, they kneel down to claim nations for His Kingdom. They are the ambassadors assigned with the call letter from above to earn souls for Jesus Christ. God has given us promise to claim nations for His glory. The intercessor's only desire is to see the earth filled with His glory.

"The earth will be filled with the knowledge of the glory of the Lord, as the waters cover the sea."

[Habakkuk 2:14]

Intercessors are given authority to claim nations for God and His ruler-ship.

"Ask of me and I will make the nations your inheritance, the ends of the earth your possession."

[Psalm 2:8]

We are called to intercede for the lost world. Having a burden for the lost souls is the greatest privilege a prayer warrior can have on this earth. The churchgoers must be aware of this truth. See how the heart of Jesus weeps. *"Jesus wept."* He did not weep for the physically bound Lazarus who had to meet his natural death after a few years. He wept for the lost souls who were spiritually bound by grave clothes. Souls, which are inwardly dead, do not know the life of eternity. Therefore, Jesus looks for intercessors who would go in search of lost souls. God is looking for one man or one woman to stand in the gap on behalf of his/her town, city and nation. What hurts His heart was that He found none.

"So I sought for a man among them who would make a wall, and stand in the gap before me on behalf of the land, that I should not destroy it; but I found no one."

[Ezekiel 22:30]

God's nature relents at His fury. He wants to see people escape from His judgment. He has the wrath to consume people like fire. He is ready to pour out His indignation on the sinful leaders of a nation or a society or a family. His soul detests the abominations of the land. He longs to see at least one man to stand at the gap to escape. It grieves His heart when He finds not a single soul who would wish to share His burden. Therefore, every believer must understand his plight and accept God's calling.

Intercessory prayer has the divine power to pull down Satan's strongholds. Paul therefore recommends the Corinthians to pray. The war with the enemy, Satan is to be fought on knees. Every church is the body of Christ, and it is called to intercede against the forces of darkness. That is the reason why Jesus made a mark of affirmation when He said,

"My house shall be called a House of Prayer for all nations."

[Mark 11:17]

Hence, every church that gives importance to prayer and fasting is a church alive with the resurrected power of Jesus Christ. A church must lead people to intercede for the nation and make them realize the power of intercessory prayer.

We pray for the lost coin, lost sheep, lost prodigal son, lost husband or lost wife, but we fail to pray for the lost nation. God is looking for the intercessors to renew their vision. Some have already lost their vision. They have willingly become entangled in the affairs of the world. The moment they wake up from their deadly stupor, they are sure to shake the nations.

We must build walls around our territory to protect our possessions and retain our goals. Usually, little children who play on the seashore build sand castles, with barracks around the castle. That would protect their castles from the oncoming waves of destruction. If the tiny tots have that much intuitive knowledge to build walls of protection to protect their little sandy castles from the raging waves, then, we should protect our loved ones from the wiles and schemes of the devil. Intercessory prayer builds walls round our loved ones, our possessions and our nation.

The heart of God found none to stand at the gap. His heart laments. He longs to see a living sacrifice. In times of war, the enemy breaks the protective city wall and makes entry into the city. Only those who are prepared to risk their lives can stand in the breach and hold back the invading troops. The master plan of the devil is to come inside and make the men inactive, paralyze their thinking and make them sit like gossiping women at the city gates. The devil tries to make its forcible entry into the city like a turbulent flood.

But when intercessors right then hold their hands and intercede for protection, claiming God's promises, the grip of the devil is released. Men in captivity are set free. The promise to every God-fearing nation is this: every first-born male child is dedicated wholly unto the Lord. The spirit of darkness can never touch what is holy. Intercessors thus stand at the breach and claim safety for their city. Satan with his army may come with a plan like a tidal wave to flood the land and wreck damage to the inhabitants; but men and women with self-sacrificing spirit form human walls and stop the entry of the enemy.

In the spiritual warfare, God calls us to play that vital role and save a city or a nation. God calls every believer. He waits for our response. He seeks a living sacrifice of one who would offer his life for his people, for his nation. He wants us to establish His kingdom on earth. Can we say with an ardent spirit like Paul?

"I will most gladly spend and be spent for your souls."

[II Corinthians 12:15]

A Model Intercessory Prayer

Prayer is an act of pouring out one's mental anguish at the feet of our heavenly Father. Most of our prayers are self-centred. Often, they are related to our own needs--physical needs, like that of a land or an ornament. God is sure to give all these extra material gifts of this earth when we first seek to establish His kingdom on earth. The seekers of these earthly blessings are the most pitiable people, because material blessings are in no way connected with eternity.

"If in this life only we have hope in Christ, we are of all men the most pitiable."

[I Corinthians 15:19]

The mission we are assigned to is greater than any other thing in this life. Then why should we limit our scope and vision?

A list of grocery items given under the pretext of a prayer request is ridiculous. God knows what we need. And we must know what He needs. God our Father graciously grants us material blessings, as we need them for our day-to-day life. However, such a list of provisions to be provided by the Sovereign Lord does not in any way disturb the enemy or the host of his kingdom. Prayer for one's need is self-centred but prayer for the souls of a nation is an unselfish act. Intercession, as an unselfish act, pleases the heart of the Father as we strive hard to establish His kingdom with the help of Jesus, the Holy Spirit and a host of angels of heaven.

God's mercy has blessed us with a bounteous supply. Instead of imploring more and more blessings to be showered on us, we can ask Him as to what we shall give to Him in return. We have been saved not by our righteous acts but by the sheer grace of God. For that great gift of salvation, we should resolutely decide to give Him back what He desires us to give. David with a heart full of gratitude says,

"What shall I render unto the Lord, for all His benefits unto me?"

[Psalm 176:12]

We must know the true living God, the Lord who holds total power over heaven and earth. He is omnipresent, present everywhere; He is omniscient, who knows everything that happens around Him. Nothing is hidden from His eyes. Everything is laid bare before His eyes. Therefore, everyone comes trembling before Him.

People must know Jesus Christ as the Son of God who bore our sins on the cross. He is the sacrificial Lamb slain for our sins. His resurrected powers still work wonders among people today. The Spirit of the Lord who dwells in the hearts of all the believers burns with a zeal to build His kingdom on earth.

Every believer who has the passion to work for His kingdom can intercede for the nation. An intercessor, by his prayer, can turn away the wrath of God from destruction. Retribution is a severe punishment of God. That punishment is kept reserved for those who commit sins of a very serious nature. The interceding prayers of the prayer-warriors can stop that impending punishment.

Daniel saw a vision – a vision of mighty power rising up. That king, who was known for his fierce features, was prospering and thriving. The king prospered by destroying the holy people. He was a cunning monarch, using deceit to prosper during his rule. He was the representative of the kingdom of deceit. Daniel was asked to seal up the vision in his mind, because it referred to the future.

In the vision Daniel saw 'the horn', the symbol of raw power, and it gave him a sickening feeling. For days, he moved with a dazed look; but no one understood it.

He resolved in his mind to fall on his knees and intercede for the nation. His first resolution was 'to set his face' toward the Lord God. He made his request 'by prayer and supplications, with fasting, sackcloth, and ashes'.

He started the prayer with a reminder of God's holy attributes. Daniel asked, 'With what tributes can I come before thy throne of mercy except to proclaim with an assurance that thou art a God of mercy?' Again, Daniel knew God is gracious to all those who keep His commandments.

Daniel identified himself with the sinners of his nation by addressing them and saying,

"We have sinned and committed iniquity; we have done wickedly and rebelled even by departing from your precepts and your judgments."

[Daniel 9:5]

He implores God to forgive his people and pardon them for having despised the prophetic words of prophets and other servants of God. He humbles himself for the sin of his people; they hardened their hearts repeatedly, but Daniel identified himself with their rebellious nature. God welcomes broken-hearted intercessors. The broken heart of an intercessor restrains the hand of God from punishing the people.

"The sacrifices of God are a broken spirit; A broken and contrite heart, O God, you will not despise."

[Psalm 51:17]

God is a God of justice when He plans to abide by His law. However, the other side of our God is Love – God is a God of love; God is a God of mercy; He is a God of compassion. He does not relish in punishing His people; rather He longs to forgive His people. If He is a God of justice on one side, He is our loving Father on the other side. Intercessors come on the scene to show us God's Fatherly role. Daniel, an effective intercessor, speaks of God's goodness and mercy:

"To the Lord our God belong mercy and forgiveness, though we have rebelled against Him."

[Daniel 9:9]

"…The Lord our God is righteous in all the work which He does…"

[Daniel 9:14]

"...I pray, let your anger and your fury be turned away from your city... and your people are a reproach to all those around us. Cause your face to shine on your sanctuary, which is desolate."

[Daniel 9:16, 17]

In his cry, he calls himself a servant and a desolate land of God left uncared. He politely reminds God of His responsibility as the land that bears His name and the people His people. For His name's sake, the retribution must be stopped, he pleads.

"...Open your eyes and see our desolations, and the city which is called by your name; for we do not present our supplications before you because of our righteous deeds, but because of your great mercies."

"O Lord, hear! O Lord, forgive! O Lord, listen and act! Do not delay for your own sake, my God, for your city and your people are called by your name."

[Daniel 9:18, 19]

Daniel's prayer brought down an angel with a word from God, a word of assurance. It was a promise of God to restore and build Jerusalem. Daniel's prayer to restore the nation brought down the chief angel Gabriel with an answer for his prayer.

Daniel had a trusting heart with a sacrificial spirit. As a true intercessor, during the time of intercessory prayer, he did not touch tasty food. He was mourning for three weeks, a period of twenty-one days.

"In those days I Daniel was mourning three full weeks. I ate no pleasant food, no meat or wine came into my mouth, nor did I anoint myself at all, till three whole weeks were fulfilled."

[Daniel 10:2, 3]

This prayer of Daniel lifted him to a higher spiritual realm. God answered him in times of great affliction. Daniel saw a vision – a great vision of the Glorious Man. Not all his doubts were cleared. However, he understood that God is in control over all things on earth. God the omnipotent rules over all power and principalities, over the visible and the invisible. God wishes to see His people 'delivered' from sins. He needs an intercessor like Daniel who earned a new title, 'O man, greatly beloved'. Daniel's intercessory prayer is an ideal model to be followed at all times.

Fasting is a Powerful Weapon

Fasting is a silent protest against an unruly government or a cruel dictator. Rulers with evil powers are to be crushed down. The excessive tyrannical strongholds are to be pulled down. The checks the tyrants keep on all sides will be removed once we take a quality decision. That decision is to pray with fasting. Moses fasted for forty days. Jesus fasted and prayed for forty days, Esther for three days and Paul for three days.

The Superior Power of God that stands on the side of the humble shatters the powers of darkness. There are only two kinds of powers or two kingdoms. The real battle is between the righteous people and the arrogant, wicked ones. The humble are ill-treated by the tyrannical minded who always love power. The power they wish to exercise on people is in the deceptive way of giving money to the weak and thereby treating them as yoked animals to plough their land. In other words, it is slavery in its worst form. Such shackles of slavery bound the Israelites when they were in Egyptian bondage. They were sinking in a muddy swamp. They did not know the ways to come out of it. They cried; they sighed; they prayed, lifting up their voice to God.

God heard their cry graciously and sent a deliverer, Moses. He rescued them from bondage and led them to the Promised Land. But, they forgot their old lives and started to rebel against God. They were ever 'a stiff-necked people'. They complained against Moses and Aaron. They were angry towards God and His ways. They made an idol of a calf and worshipped it, saying that the idol rescued them from the cruel hands of the Pharaoh. It was an abomination in the eyes of God. Their callous and hardened nature provoked God's wrath. Many died on their way to their promised land. Moses prostrated before the Lord for forty days and forty nights because the Lord had said that He would destroy the people. He intercedes thus:

"Therefore I prayed to the Lord, and said: "O Lord God, do not destroy your people and your inheritance whom you have redeemed through your greatness, whom you have brought out of Egypt with a mighty hand."

[Deuteronomy 9:26]

In the New Testament days after the arrival of Jesus, we were given a silent weapon to fight against the powers of evil. When fasting is added with prayer, it turns out to be the right weapon to shatter the powers of evil. Jesus Himself has said that this kind of devil will never come out without fasting.

"However, this kind does not go out except by prayer and fasting."

[Matthew 17:21]

If Jesus propagates fasting, then there must be some real truth in it. We cannot question it or doubt it. We must put our total trust in Him and His principle. What is the secret behind this piece of advice? Why should Jesus be keen to propagate this principle of prayer and fasting?

Jesus is the ambassador from the kingdom of God. He knows all the principles followed in a king's court. When He says fasting is the key to unlock the treasures of heaven, then immediately we decide to follow His guidance until we get the desired result. God honours implicit obedience. Most people missed their goals by questioning and arguing. They have already lost their vision. Instead of joining such doubting groups let us keep moving to rescue people from the clutches of the devil. Our calling is to establish His kingdom on earth.

We are given a great commission to destroy evil and unfurl the banner of victory in the territory we are allotted to rule. His chosen ambassadors have to fight a brave battle to the end. In this spiritual warfare, we are mere instruments in His hands. Rightly, Samuel has said,

"Then all this assembly shall know the Lord does not save with sword and spear; for the battle is the Lord's and he will give all of you (Philistines) in our hands."

[I Samuel 17:47]

Hence, we carry on our Lord's work with faith and courage, and with a sense of certainty. God has not given us the spirit of fear; but He has given us a mind with great power.

Let us imagine a picture. You are in battle, standing with a drawn sword in your hand; the sword you hold moves here and there, attacking the foes. You simply stand, holding the sword in your hand. An unseen supernatural force, an angel of mighty power is moving your sword by standing behind you. This is like a computer-generated graphic picture you should always keep in your mind. Thus, we are ordained to achieve accomplishment after accomplishment for His kingdom.

To whom does God send a host of angels to assist? Only to those who take a resolution to live by faith. That demands total faith in God. The righteous shall live by faith.

"Behold the proud, His soul is not upright in him; But the just shall live by his faith."

[Habakkuk 2:4]

One who derives extraordinary faith in His promise is ever successful. Most extraordinary leaders were seen ordinary in the beginning of their career. Moses admitted his shortcoming in the plainest terms possible that he was a stammering person:

"Then Moses said to the Lord, 'O my Lord, I am not eloquent, neither before nor since you have spoken to your servant; but I am slow of speech and slow of tongue.'"

[Exodus 4:10]

Such a stammering person was chosen to stand equal before a king, the powerful Pharaoh; a man with stammering turned out to be a great deliverer! Joshua, his successor, comes out victoriously holding on to the promise of faith he was given by the Lord.

"Be strong and of good courage; do not be afraid, nor be dismayed, For the Lord your God is with you wherever you go."

[Joshua 1:9]

Barak was too timid to take up a fight against Sisera, the tyrant. Deborah has to appear by giving inspiration to him, which in turn makes him say:

"If you will go with me, then I will go; but if you will not go with me, I will not go."

[Judges 4:9]

The story ends with a victory in battle. God subdued the tyrant. The angel of the Lord has to appear and infuse courage into timid Gideon saying:

"The Lord is with you, mighty man of valour!"

[Judges 6:12]

A new title is given to the meek Gideon to make new conquests. God's ways are innumerable and His choices of leaders are incomprehensible. An ordinary shepherd boy,

David was chosen to put an end to the giant Goliath. The same shepherd boy, David was inspired to write a book of Psalms for God's glory. He has a fast-moving pen in His hand.

"My heart is overflowing with a good theme; I recite my composition concerning the King…"

[Psalm 45:1]

Esther is a soft bird, shut forever in a golden cage. She was living under constant threats and fear. Any attempt she makes against the king's law will bring instant death upon her. With a feeble heart, she sends the message:

"Any man or woman who goes into the inner court to the king, who has not been called, he has but one law: put to death…"

[Esther 4:11]

This timid girl receives a set of inspiring words with a tinge of admonition from her uncle Mordecai:

"Do not think in your heart that you will escape in the king's palace any more than all the other Jews. For if you remain completely silent at this time, relief and deliverance will arise for the Jews from another place, but you and your father's house will perish."

[Esther 4:13, 14]

The word 'perish' makes her take a quality decision right then. By risking her life, the goal has to be achieved, she realizes. She collects her maids to fast and pray. Fasting is the silent weapon of protest against hard hearts. It is the only weapon against the forces of evil. It gives innate courage to the one who fasts and prepares him to accomplish hard tasks. Fasting helps Esther to turn humble before heaven's doors with those maids. They humbled themselves down to earth; it spoke about their utter helpless state; she prostrated herself almost like a hunted bird, pleading before the great Saviour. Fasting means we can do nothing by our own effort; it is like admitting that we are powerless. Fasting lifts the hand of the omnipotent to intervene and defend the powerless.

The very decision 'to fast' gives Esther the courage to risk her life. She is no more the old hunted bird. Instead, she rises to become a glorious picture of courage – 'a profile of courage'. Note her words – how powerful they are! With what authority she gives the command to the messengers of Mordechai! She stands as an ambassador of the invisible kingdom of God with a resolute mind to rout wicked Haman and his inhuman schemes. What echoes in her mind is – "When God is with me, who can come against me?"

Although God allows the wicked to flourish for a while and offers them chances to repent, He always warns them and opposes them as long as they persist in their wickedness. Esther's most authoritative words are: *"Go gather all the Jews who are present in Shushan and fast for me; neither eat nor drink for three days, night or day. My maids and I will fast likewise. And so I will go to the king, which is against the law; and if I perish, I perish!"*

[Esther 4:16]

The story of Esther ends with a note of victory. Peals of laughter and jubilation run through the streets. The God-fearing people, celebrating the victory over the Godless pagans, hoist the banner of victory up.

How did this all happen? Esther declared a national fast to all the Jews. There was urgency in her call. She understood her high calling. She chose a select group of maids to fast and pray. God's hand moves when people in prayer kneel down before His throne of mercy. They lift their hands towards heaven; lifting up one's hands is a symbolic act of one's total surrender before the sovereign Lord. They have no one in the world except God who can fight for them.

There is a popular Indian story related to the theme of timidity. There was a mouse that got frightened of everything. Therefore, it expressed its fear to a magician. The magician, out of pity, changed it into a cat. It was running around happily. It happened to see a dog, got frightened, and came back to the magician. He changed the cat into a dog. Again, it got frightened on seeing a tiger. The magician changed it into a tiger. When it saw a hunter, it came back with fear to the magician. This time, the magician did not change it into a hunter; but he changed it once again into a mouse saying, *"I changed you into a tiger – a ferocious animal of the forest; but still you have the timid heart of a mouse."*

This simple story makes us think. If we rationally analyse, we will understand that the shortcoming is in us and it does not come from external sources or from anyone outside. God gives us courage and confidence to face the challenges of the world. Courage in us is to be tapped with the help of Jesus Christ who gave Himself on the Cross to redeem us. His holy blood has power to give us victory over Satan. And Satan and his army are defeated by God on the Cross. Men and women, therefore have to claim this victory in His blood and march on to defeat all their negative beliefs, fears and depression. The Lord has a hope, a perfect plan, and a future for you and me. To fill us with that hope, God the Father has given His only begotten son, Jesus Christ to be crucified on the Cross. Note how Jeremiah gives us the words of hope:

"For I know the plans I have for you," declares the Lord, "plans to prosper you and not to harm you, plans to give you hope and a future."

[Jeremiah 29:11]

God has a wonderful plan for us all. These plans give us a hope and a future.

When we seek to do well with a determined mind, we are on the winning side of God. When I repeatedly say, "Surely He will do well," the devil gets tired of me and leaves my body, my house and me. I open the door for Him to enter my house because His plan for me in my life is perfect.

God detests the hearts that are hardened against His people. It is an abomination in the eyes of God. The land is full of such abominations. God's people have to gather like an army to fight against these evils.

People we see around us are mostly egoists; they cannot tolerate the slightest trace of their ego being faintly touched or eroded. They are, in other words, lovers of power. They must rule people, especially God-fearing people. The Pharaoh's heart was hardened against God's people. Every time he hardened, it brought forth the glory of God. It is a vain effort to stand against God and His people. Knowing it well, the Pharaoh was still refusing the demands of God's people. In every one of his attempts, the Pharaoh met with failure – plague after plague was the net result he saw. In spite of all that, he hardened his heart. Why? To bring forth glory to God's name!

The Pharaoh's hardened heart was on one side; the sighs and tears of His people were on the other side. The Red Sea before the people, and their frightened clamour were on one side; the Egyptian army was on the other side. The people looked pressed on all sides. In truth, they were not. God made the water to split and rise as walls for His people to pass through and the same waters drowned the Egyptian chariots and the Pharaoh's soldiers. What does it show? Out of the hard heart of the Pharaoh, God comes to show His glory. His name is exalted.

The devil keeps busy, spinning a large web. The moment a spider catches a fly in its web, it injects paralyzing venom into the victim. The more the poison the victim receives, the more it finds it difficult to move, think or act. It is ever under the control of that poisonous spider.

In a similar vein, the devil starts to spin a network programme. The demonic power moves from one person to another. First it begins in a small circle of friends or a family; in an organization it occupies a wider and larger level. Gradually it grips all the people and keeps an entire organization under its control. This is how a family or a nation is yoked under demonic control, a modern-day bondage to satanic power. What is the part of a believer's role here? What methods should he adopt to rescue his people from the snares of the devil? Let us analyse.

Know thy Enemy – Expose His War Weapons

Jesus, through His life and teaching, has shown us the devil and his activities. Satan attacked Jesus and that spiritual warfare throws more light on the devil's battle plans. Satan remains the great deceiver and he waits for every new opportunity to destroy human relationships. The war weapons he uses are jealousy, bitterness, selfishness and resentment. There is no wonder why many families are living in separation. He is ever a destroyer, destroying peace and joy. Satan is described as a liar and destroyer of life; Jesus, on the other hand, comes as the Giver of abundant life to man.

"The thief does not come except to steal, and to kill, and to destroy. I have come that they may have life, and that they may have it more abundantly."

[John 10:10]

Often we are led astray, not knowing who our enemy is. For a wife, a husband is not her enemy. Parents! Say it aloud, "Children are not our enemies!" For children, parents are not their enemies. Then who is their enemy? Obviously, the one common enemy to all of them is devil.

Satan with all his wiles and schemes sows seeds of discord and disharmony. The main motive of the devil is to make husband and wife disagree with each other; or children and parents disagree with one another. Largely, we see this in society or in a nation. Why did Jesus say that He brings separation in the same household, when He Himself is called the Prince of Peace? Why then, is there discord in one's own household?

The answer: All are expected to live in His faith. If there is division in their faith, there will be division among people. Not a single person should waver in his faith.

In Joshua's simple words faith is:

"But as for me and my house, we will serve the Lord."

[Joshua 24:15]

Satan very cleverly attacks people with his new strategies. Satan executes plans but those plans, we ought to know, are permitted by God. God, we see, allows evil to move in its own way; it moves mysteriously to meet its own tragic end. Everything is in perfect control under God's power. Therefore, the battle is the Lord's and the final victory is to be celebrated by us.

Let us focus on God, the Father's glory and majesty, and the coming of His kingdom in power here on earth as it is in heaven. How do we fight with the spirits of darkness to bring His kingdom on earth? We should know our position and stand firm, as our Lord asks us.

King Hezekiah says:

"Be strong and courageous; do not be afraid or discouraged because of the king of Assyria and the vast army with him, for there is a greater power with us than with him. With him is only the arm of flesh, but with us is the Lord our God to help us and to fight our battles."

[II Chronicles 32:7-8]

See how Jahaziel encouraged King Jehoshaphat and his army when the Spirit of the Lord came upon him:

"Listen..." This is what the Lord says to you: "Do not be afraid or discouraged because of this vast army. For the battle is not yours, but God's.

...You will not have to fight this battle. Take up your positions; stand firm and see the deliverance the Lord will give you...

Do not be afraid; do not be discouraged. Go out to face them tomorrow, and the Lord will be with you."

[II Chronicles 20:15, 17]

The warfare weapons of the devil are fear, discouragement, hatred and deception. For everything original, there is a counterfeit. The devil easily captures the minds of young and old by introducing some deceptive products. It is one of his favourite methods; he introduces somebody close to the original and after some time, he breaks the value of that genuine person. Sometimes, even in the food we are served, we find deceptive food. King Solomon warns people not to be tempted by deceptive food, lest we shall lose our gracious words.

"Do not eat the bread of a miser. Nor desire his delicacies,

For as he thinks in his heart, so is he. The morsel you have eaten, you will vomit up, and waste your pleasant words."

[Proverbs 23:6-8]

Similarly, there is deceptive money transaction in every occupation – giving money to someone as though out of mercy and friendship outwardly, while lodging in the heart of hearts, a wicked scheme to ruin the life of the innocent. Many have already fallen into such snares. Satan cleverly makes his entry in every area of man's life. The final plan of Satan is to plunge people into despair and disillusionment, sickness and loss of peace. See how Paul admonishes:

"Let no one cheat you. See to it that no one takes you captive through hollow and deceptive philosophy."

[Colossians 2:8]

The present-day cult theories introduced into the world are meant to mislead believers. These theories are fabricated ones; they may be pleasing to the world but rejected by the Lord. If we have all fullness in Christ, we shall never go in for empty philosophy. For every genuine product or principle or belief, man wants to find a substitute. Believers must know that such craving is given by the devil. The substitute is from the spoiler, the destroyer; it is not from God.

In most of the religious meetings today, more time is allotted for skits, dances, games, drama, gymnastic exercises, and so forth – all imported products of modern culture! By the time they come to the session of hearing the word of God, they sit exhausted, wriggling in their seats. Spiritual meetings end up as the activities of a club, with tea and snacks! Satan does not bother as long as young men and women leap and shout in joy.

Bringing passivity into man's thinking process is Satan's ultimate goal; all kinds of imitative methods of the world are copies, and they are supplied to the youth in order to lure them into his trap. Satan is in no way disturbed, and he is happy as long as people are not ready for the word of God.

Satan allows people to give tithe; he is not in the least disturbed when they are obeying God's commandment; because he knows the trick of keeping the same people under his captivity, in certain other areas like driving them to bribery, or making them live corrupt and immoral lives.

People think that money gives them power. Today it has become a mighty world-ruling power. The devil wants to rule the people by giving them the temptation to grab others' money. Money can be used to ease the burden imposed on the poor and to support orphans and widows. However, Satan changes their mind and turns their attention for his own selfish and unholy purposes. Satan, in fact, allures men to covetousness.

"For the love of money is the root of all kinds of evil, for which some have strayed from the faith in their greediness, and pierced themselves through with many sorrows."

[I Timothy 6:10]

The hearts of people are so hardened that they go to any extreme – the extreme of committing murder for gain. Advertisements fetch money for a magazine. However, can a Christian magazine endorse unholy products? Is it right to promote such sales? Believers do it because they are not aware of the traps laid underneath.

Another dirty swamp, into which we unknowingly fall, is the state of stupor. We do not even know whether we live or not. The mind of man is turned to passivity. By consuming numerous cheap products, man has numbed his senses. As long as man is lulled to such a sleepy state, the kingdom of Satan gets enlarged. Jesus Christ repeatedly tells his disciples to 'watch and pray' and 'pray with fasting'.

Often we hear: *"...the spirit indeed is willing, but the flesh is weak."*

[Matthew 26:4]

Man must struggle to come out from this drowsy state. He must know the will of God and the purpose of his life. Satan blinds men by not allowing them to find out their purpose in life, because purpose gives hope to man in life. A preacher shares word of faith, hope, and purpose while Satan cleverly tricks to lull the people to sleep.

Satan will always raise a group of false propagandists as his agents; his aim is to thwart the plan of the genuine leaders; he will spread false rumours about the genuine followers of Christ. People thrown into confusion will believe rumours. This is how Satan tries to succeed in stopping religious activities. He is a father of lies.

Since Satan is the prince of demons, he loves to create his own battles. He will battle against fasting, intercessory prayers, messages about the Second Coming and repentance. He will make every attempt to stop prayers or change them into ineffective ones. He produces sleep and weakness among prayer warriors. He achieves success at times by making the leaders feel lonely, defeated or discouraged; he lands them in despair. Some leaders, in course of time, lose their vision and start working in the opposite direction. Religious meeting halls are turned into educational centres!

A man like Job was tried in sickness. Paul was given a thorn, which was ever painful to his body. Some of the disciples of Jesus were put in prisons. They were chained with fetters because their souls could not be shackled or broken.

We see Satan pictured as a roaring lion, roaming around to devour the believers. However, in the midst of all these trials, we have a ray of hope; we see a river flowing through His wounds – a river of the precious blood of Jesus Christ – His mighty power flowing and strengthening us. We have seen the fullness of God who lived, died and resurrected with a glorious body. Knowing that fully well, we need not go in for counterfeits. Moreover, He made Himself as an atonement sacrifice for the sins of the people (Hebrews 1:17). This great sacrifice took away the wrath of God. God's wrath was turned away by the great intercessor Jesus Christ, because of whom man's weaknesses change into strength.

Remember, Satan with all his evil designs is a defeated foe. God's greatest power is released when we affirm His promise given by Jesus:

"Behold, I give unto you power to tread on serpents and scorpions, and over all the power of the enemy; and nothing shall by any means hurt you."

[Luke 10:19]

The truth is that we gain victory only through the very devices that are used by Satan. All his evil deeds, at the end, work together for our good.

"And we know that all things work together for good to those who love God, to those who are called according to His purpose."

[Romans 8:28]

Let us not get entangled with the affairs of the world – the snares like hatred, enmity, resentment or fear. The day we confess our sins and turn away from them, we receive forgiveness. Similarly, whatever wrongs people have done against us, we can easily forgive since our minds have travelled a long journey to the mount of transfiguration. Our thought patterns are completely transformed because we know that the common enemy to man is not man, it is the devil. Peace and harmony are restored once we confess our sins.

Once we come to know of Satan and his ways, the enemy and his attributes, we can win the battle. What we need most is discernment. This is the gift God wants to give us, His believers.

The Work of the Sovereign Lord

There may be moments of despair when the intercessor finds no favourable sign of release for his captives. Those loveless moments may be numerous, and they may lead him to kneel down with a sinking heart to cry unto Him: *"What is the use of praying for those dead souls? When are they going to be renewed in their spirit? These are the people who have no desire for real blessing."* Moses had the birth pangs when he cried unto the Lord, "Am I the one who gave birth to these people." Paul too likens the intercessor's prayer to birth pangs.

An intercessor need not land in such despair. A total transformation or a change in the heart of a sinner is to be brought by the sovereign will of God.

This work is not mine or yours. The Lord can do that marvellous work in a person in his own marvellous way, at His own marvellous timing. His promises are true. Note how keen He is to accomplish His promises:

"Call unto me, and I will answer thee, and show thee great and mighty things, which thou knowest not."

[Jeremiah 38:3]

The greatest mediator for every prisoner is Jesus Christ. He does the priestly job for every sinner – interceding for the prisoner, and showing His holy blood as the atonement sacrifice to His father in heaven. The recreating power of the crucified transforms a sinner wonderfully. The abject slavery is broken in an unmistakable term. The prisoner will be freed from his captivity; he will be freed from his craving for drugs or drinks; sin no longer attracts him. When the word of God takes deep roots in him, he becomes more fruitful to others. This is another miraculous aspect of God's ways. His sacrificial blood cleanses the sinner, breaks his addictions and makes him whole.

All glory to Jesus; His word, His blood works rejuvenation in the mind of a captive. An intercessor, in spite of all his travails and cries, has no right to share an atom of glory for himself. A prayer warrior must be willing to become the most insignificant marl of dust in the world. People may label him as filth and squalor of the earth. However, he can draw satisfaction that he could serve humanity just as salt would make food tasty. Salt, we know, remains hidden in delicious dishes, but it adds taste to every food item.

Similarly, an intercessor remains hidden behind his closed prayer closet, making his supplication to our Father in heaven. He has no name. Nor does he ever seek fame. A tiny violet flower, half hidden behind a bush, is a beautiful creation of God. As it grows hidden, it cannot give joy to a passer-by. But to God, its creator, it gives immense joy.

An intercessor fasts and prays for the lost souls of the world. Though not recognized by the world, he is well appreciated and loved by our heavenly Father. Here on earth he goes unnoticed, unsung, and unhonoured. However, he deserves a reward, and it is on the way, when the Lord Jesus comes back in all glory. Great will be God's reward, because the intercessor shares the burden of our Father's heart.

A great sacrifice was made by the Lamb – Jesus Christ, the son of God who came down in the person of flesh, word being made flesh. By His great sacrifice, He has appeased the wrath of God. Man's sins deserve punishment, but,

"According to the Law, almost all things are purified with blood, and without shedding of blood there is no remission."

[Hebrews 9:22]

In the Old Testament days, a high priest entered the most holy place every year with the blood of an animal. But Jesus appeared to put away sin by sacrificing Himself. He has entered the most Holy place – a place not built by human hands – He entered into heaven itself, now to reappear again as our God.

For this reason, He is called the mediator of the new covenant. He has redeemed us through His own death. There is no redemption for transgression without the mediator. Those who are called will receive the promise of the eternal inheritance only through Him and by Him. The promise is confirmed in the following verse:

"Therefore, He is also able to save to the uttermost those who come to God through Him, since He always lives to make intercession for them."

[Hebrews 7:25]

We have such a high priest, a High Mediator who is seated at the right hand of the throne of the Majesty in the heavens. A priest, in the time of Moses, entered the tabernacle through a veil. Today we are consecrated to enter the Holy place by the blood of Jesus and through the veil, which is His flesh.

Having sat down on the throne next to His father to intercede for us, He looks at man's miserable condition on earth and pleads for his redemption. In Jesus, God has given us a great comforter who prays with a winning attitude. He is the third person among the Triune God. When He comes to move hearts, He moves them mightily – a revival fire comes to sweep through the land. The outpouring of God's spirit brings forth a torrential rain in the midst of people. The revival fires start to burn out sins at several places.

We do not know how to pray and intercede for our own loved ones. For we do not know the perfect will of God on their lives. You have to see that they too inherit eternity. People around us should not lose their chance to inherit eternal life. For which they have to act and live according to the will of God. Therefore, the intercessors first pray for the will of God.

When you are called to intercede for others, then you ascertain that your calling is a high calling that comes from the Lord. You may be despised by the people, but be sure that your work is pleasing in the eyes of God. Build up your own spiritual power by praying in the Holy Spirit. When the Holy Spirit stirs up in you, you do not settle for lower things; but you move up higher and higher into a place that God has prepared for you. You shall be a great blessing upon your entire household, to the church and in your own town. People can see you walk amidst the anointed, speak and deliver messages in the anointed spirit of God. They will know it is God's spirit that speaks to them. The spirit of God prays to God through sighs and groans. The great intercessor for every believer is the Spirit of God.

"Likewise, the spirit also helps in our weaknesses. For we do not Know what we should pray for as we ought, but the spirit Himself makes intercession for us with groaning which cannot be uttered."

[Romans 8:26, 27]

Mediators generally end up paying a very high price. The price is usually an expensive one, which cannot be compensated. They risk dangers willingly in order to save people from the oncoming indignation of God. They stand between man and God. Moses ever stood at the gap between his people and God, interceding for God's people. He was ready to see his name taken out from the book of God. Daniel was thrown into a lion's den; Jeremiah the prophet was thrown into a cistern for months; Esther happily risked her life to save her people by standing before the king, unmindful of the danger.

When the intercessors take one step forward, God in an extraordinary way pulls them up through deep waters. He gives them more courage and confidence to fight for the perishing souls. An intercessor enjoys a sense of calm serenity even in perilous moments. No external force or situation disturbs him.

They enjoy innate peace even while standing at the war front. For Deborah and Barak, the battleground turns out to be a place of praise and worship; for Paul and Silas, a prison becomes a praise and worship hall; for Peter, jail is a resting place to go into a deep undisturbed slumber, even at the very moment of death. They are ever cheerful and encourage others to be cheerful. Such marvellous fortitude of these intercessory prayer warriors make people search the Scripture for Gospel truth. As they have already met with great loss, their prayers become ardent and effective. Prayers that spring from a sincere heart bring the heavens down. Whenever God sees one innocent and saintly person, the spirit of God descends mightily to overthrow the powers of darkness and the forces of evil.

The great burden of intercessors is to bring many sons and daughters to God's kingdom. The Father's only wish is to redeem people to the fold of Jesus Christ who died on the cross so that humanity will be released from the fear of death. Therefore, deliverance for man is through Jesus Christ.

"Inasmuch then as the children are partners of flesh and blood, He Himself likewise shared in the same; that through death He might destroy him who had the power of death, that is, the devil, and release those who through fear of death were all their lifetime subject to bondage."

[Hebrews 2:14, 15]

Every kind of bondage is being cut asunder by Jesus, the Bondage-Breaker. He knows what suffering is and what bondage means. Man's temptation is not anything new to Jesus. He himself had walked through the path of temptation; He came down to us in flesh and blood

"Because He himself suffered when He was tempted, He is able to help those who are being tempted."

[Hebrews 2:18]

Why His own people were made captives? Was the Lord responsible for it? Why were the people of Israel in exile and remained forsaken? Whose fault was it? Who was responsible for this? The only answer is this: Israel was to be blamed for its inequities.

"For your iniquities, you have sold yourselves, and for your transgressions, your mother has been put away."

[Isaiah 50:1, 2]

It grieves the heart of the Lord to see His own chosen ones bound in bondage. As a father of compassion, He has to act as a God of Justice. There is none to redeem them.

However, this is a people robbed and plundered; all of them are snared in holes; and they are hidden in prison houses; they are for prey, and no one delivers; for plunder, and no one says, "Restore!"

[Isaiah 42:22]

Jacob was given for plunder and Israel was given to the robbers. Because they sinned against Him and they would not walk in His ways. As a judge, He inflicts punishment when the period of tribulation is over, once again, He shows compassion to His people. He has framed the laws and therefore He cannot break His own laws. That is the reason why people are bound in shackles for a period of a few years. Daniel understood the number of years people would undergo pain. The word of the Lord was revealed through Jeremiah, the prophet, about the events that He would accomplish. It would be a time of trouble for Judah and Jerusalem. The city and the temple would be destroyed. There is no other God besides Him – a just God and a compassionate Saviour. A prey can never be taken from the hand of a mighty person.

Thus says the Lord, *"Even the captives of the mighty shall be taken away. And the prey of the terrible be delivered; for I shall contend with him who contends with you; and I will save your children… All flesh shall know that I, the Lord am your Saviour, And your Redeemer, the Mighty one of Jacob."*

[Isaiah 49:25, 26]

Thus, God fulfilled the promises of Israel's restoration that He had previously given. The promises were given to people through the prophets Isaiah and Jeremiah. God immediately brings proper judgment upon people who treated His people harshly. Jehovah brought judgment upon the king of Babylon and his people because they stood in the way of God's people when they returned to Jerusalem to rebuild the temple.

Even a great king like Nebuchadnezzar was cleared from the path, when he stood as a barrier from building the temple of God. God wants a sanctuary to dwell in with His people. He delights to dwell with them when they praise and worship Him. Anyone who denies a sanctuary to God is cleared off from the path.

The same God brought another set of people to show mercy and love to the oppressed Israelites. God chose Cyrus to show love and compassion to His people. They were used as instruments of restoration for the Israelites. In all these historical events, one fine fabric is interwoven in the interior work. We see the same flowering pattern in every event where God intervened to save His people. Whenever God's people turn away from His ways, God in turn leaves them in the hands of cruel rulers. It may extend over a period of twenty to thirty years, or at times, even longer. God's people, usually at the end, cry out in despair claiming God's mercy. They sit, repent and pray for His grace. They repeatedly proclaim. "The Lord is good and His mercy endures forever." God in His ultimate wisdom clears the barriers and paves the path for His people to walk upon. He removes power from a tyrant and hands over the kingship to a God-fearing leader. Sometimes the heart of a cruel man is changed in a miraculous way. He begins to show care and concern to God's people. Saul, the persecutor of Christians, was touched by the Lord marvellously, and thereby he began to work under the name Paul. Since then, Paul the apostle of Christ began to preach the Gospel.

A corrupt establishment may work at crossroads to defame Christian faith. Incompetent governments may work against Christians and oppress them to deny their Christian belief. Christians placed in these situations are asked not to oppose the government; instead they must be told to obey their authorities. When the believers gather, fast and pray, then God changes the destiny of a government. When we humble ourselves before God, God intervenes and brings a change in the entire pattern of man's rule on earth. Esther changed the Jewish decree; Haman is not the choice of God. Haman and his household were destroyed by the new Jewish law.

God expects Christians to stand against rulers who love power. The only weapon is our prayer, a silent but powerful one, which comes from the deepest depths of our heart. It is not in God's plan to give pre-eminence to evil rulers. His plan is to bring them down and manifest His glory by destroying them. God enthrones a just ruler who rules people in the fear of God. David the king, who was a man after God's heart, speaks about God's desire:

"He that ruleth over men must be just, ruling in the fear of God."

[II Samuel 23:2]

Allowing ourselves to work submissively under a tyrant is a sin, because it is bondage built by our own choice. In truth, it is a kind of total surrender to intimidation. The anointing power of our Lord is ready to break the yokes. Indeed, we are not chosen to subject ourselves to captivity. We must set ourselves free from the cruel oppression created by sinful forces. It was a sin on the part of the Pharaoh, who had an evil desire to control the lives of Israelites, for he treated them as slaves. It was also a sin on the part of Israelites who submitted themselves to be kept in bondage by a cruel task-master. When a God-fearing leader is raised up to rule, blessings shall follow on the lives of the ruled.

Man is born free, but by his own ignorance, he has courted the devil and his chains. Man, because of his lack of knowledge, has lost his vision. As the proverbial saying goes, "Where there is no vision, people will perish." Let us join, rebuild His kingdom, and establish it on earth for His glory. Let His banner of love be unfurled everywhere. Let the captor and the captive be set free to enjoy the fresh air of freedom, another new heaven here on earth.

Here is yet another awesome thing to note. The deliverer and the people to be delivered are knit, strangely enough, in a mysterious bond. Moses, the deliverer with the captive Israelites, was moving towards Canaan. Esther identified herself with the Jewish race; Jeremiah with his people, Daniel with his exiles; Job with his friends; the apostle Paul travailed with the Holy Spirit for the redemption of the whole of humanity. Remember, God intervenes to show forth His glory by taking His people to cross the Red Sea, and commanding the same sea-waters to devour the

Egyptian army of the Pharaoh. Before God's intervention, the captives must be set free.

Every believer inherits God's grace that will redeem the sinners from captivity. The believer is advised by Paul to avoid foolish and ignorant ways of counselling, for they may generate strife. When we approach the captives in humility, God will show them His love and truth, and make them repent for their sins. Ultimately, it is truth that will set them free.

Now that you have been set free from sin and having become slaves of God, the benefit you reap leads to holiness, and the result is eternal life.

[Romans 6:22]

Praise pulls down Barriers and brings Victory

When repentance is made for the wrongs we have done, then it brings divine protection to us. We become God's people. God's warning to the Israelites was not to take any cursed thing from Jericho. God had warned them thus:

"I will not be with you any more unless you destroy whatever among you is doomed to destruction… You cannot stand against your enemies until you remove it."

[Joshua 7:12-13]

God's commandment is not to covet the other man's property. It leads us to disaster. The devil has the legal right to have its hold on those stolen goods. Achan listened to the temptations and retained God-forbidden things with him.

God cannot tolerate this double kind of allegiance. Achan's direct disobedience to God brought disaster on that day.

Jealousy is the outcome of one's own low self-esteem; its underlying cause is the desire for worth. People who are tormented by jealousy are often hurled into an emotion of insecurity. When they recognize jealousy in them, they need to come forward with repentance to the person concerned. When we mistrust somebody, we can pray with a person whom we trust. God, then, will graciously heal all the areas of insecurity.

Other emotions which sap our inner peace are worry, anxiety and fear. We worry, fret and fume about unborn tomorrow; instead of trusting Him for everything, we worry about everything – it may be about our forthcoming examination or the interview we have to attend for a job or the prolonged illness of a loved one. In all such anxious moments, we are asked to stand still with God and ask Him to fill us with His peace. We have to hand over our fear and anxiety and get back His presence of peace. One needs to brush aside fear and anxiety and start praising God. A wonderful weapon here is praise.

Paul advises the Philippians as follows:

"Be anxious for nothing; but in everything by prayer and supplication, with thanksgiving, let your requests be made known to God."

[Philippians 4:6]

The imprisonment of Paul and Silas at the prison of Philippi brings a wonderful message from the Book of

Acts. Prison house changes into a praise house! Paul and Silas were flogged and thrown into prison. However, at midnight…? What happened at midnight? Something, which you and I can never imagine or expect – they were praising God! At midnight, Paul and Silas were praying and singing hymns to God, and the prisoners were listening to them.

Suddenly there was a great earthquake, so that the foundations of the prison were shaken; and immediately all the doors were opened and everyone's chains were loosened. [Acts 16:25, 26]

They exalted the name of God where His name was blasphemed. They had total trust in Him and that gave them joy to pray and praise. Anyone in their state would have indulged in self-pity; or they would have started to wail and complain. "Lord I did your work; but see what you've done!" However, Paul and Silas did not see their external circumstances. Instead, they derived strength from their spiritual inner source. They did not wait for intervention from a human hand. They were persecuted for a noble cause – the work they carried out for their Master. They believed that God had to send judgment for persecution. Because, the battle is the Lord's. He is the author and finisher of faith. They waited for Divine intervention. That made them pray and sing hymns to God. 'Hymns' are 'songs of praise'.

God's ways are unfathomable. God in His own tremendous power, caused an earthquake; the foundations of the very prison where His servants were imprisoned started to shake; all the prison doors wherein they were shut, opened immediately. Man's hand bound them with chains. But God's hand loosened their chains.

The damp dungeon of the prison with its strong foundation, closed doors and iron shackles could not stand before God's presence. When 'God comes, revival comes' along with God. When God comes, tremendous things happen. Isaiah 64 verses 1 and 2 refer to God's arrival:

Oh, that thou wouldst rend the heavens and come down, that the mountains might flow down at thy presence… that the nations may tremble at thy presence.

Again, on the day of Pentecost, suddenly there came a sound from heaven as of a rushing mighty wind and it filled the entire house where they were sitting. [Acts 2:12]

A mighty change occurs in the jailor who is in charge of Paul and Silas. *"What shall we do?"* the jailor asked. *"Believe in the Lord Jesus Christ, and you will be saved, you and your household,"* replied Paul and Silas. Overnight, the jailor's house turned into a tabernacle for God to dwell in. They accepted the Lord; they washed the stripes of Paul and Silas; they set food before the two servants of God.

The story ends with a warm reception that was given by the persecutors to the persecuted. What we remember here is this: it was Paul who was once persecuting the Christians! That transformation from persecution to praise in Paul was wrought by the marvellous touch of the Lord Himself. Praise be to our Lord and Saviour Jesus Christ.

Another notable feature here is – praise flows from the heart that has been deeply hurt and wounded; spirit that has been crushed; body that has been slashed by whipping and beatings. The devil fills his agents with hatred who in turn torture His chosen disciples. That is the reason why

His chosen ones willingly endure hardships. They are hated and punished by the people of the world. The world treats them cruelly because of their religious beliefs. His disciples happily endure persecution and, wherever they go, they preach the Gospel. Where the Gospel is preached, the kingdom of the devil is disturbed. The agents of Satan are filled with the same emotions of Satan – emotions like hatred and anger; they are keen to lift His disciples to the cross. These disciples, having known their beliefs in Christ, rejoice while they suffer. They bless those who persecute them. (Romans 12:14)

Jesus had already alerted them saying, "They persecuted me, they will persecute you," (John 15:20). And so, *"…a great persecution broke out against the church," (Acts 8:1). Paul gladly says, "When we are persecuted, we will endure it."* (I Corinthians 4:12)

The persecutors of Peter and other apostles were furious and wanted to put them to death. They were filled with jealousy. They took the apostles to Sanhedrin and had them flogged. Then they ordered them not to speak in the name of Jesus, and let them go. They were flogged; there were plans devised to put them to death; they were strictly warned not to speak the Gospel; but they were keen on spreading the Gospel!

The persecution was on one side. Immediately after persecution, there was joy with praise on the other side. See how the apostles rejoice:

The apostles left the Sanhedrin, rejoicing because they had been counted worthy of suffering disgrace for the Name. Day after day, in the temple courts, and from house to house, they never stopped teaching and proclaiming the good news, that Jesus is the Christ. [Acts 5:41, 42]

Another kind of persecutors enjoy sending false rumours and slanderous reports about godly men and women. Their envious nature makes them issue wrong statements. There is a proverbial saying that runs like this: only a tree which bears ripe fruits will receive hits by sharp stones. Similarly, God's people are at the receiving end for sharp remarks. They, who are reviled at by persecutors, undergo mental anguish and shed tears in agony.

Jesus gives a word of exhortation to His people who pass through such bitter experiences:

"Blessed are you when people insult you, persecute you, and falsely say all kinds of evil against you because of Meme. Rejoice and be glad, because great is your reward in heaven, for in the same way they persecuted the prophets who were before you."

[Matthew 5:11, 12]

"But I say unto you, love your enemies, bless them that curse you, do good to them that hate you, and pray for them who spitefully use you and persecute you."

[Matthew 5:44]

"Yea and all that desire to live godly in Christ Jesus shall suffer persecution."

[II Timothy 3:12]

Praise from Paul and Silas brought salvation to an entire household of the persecutor. But in the case of the persecutor, King Herod, there was the supernatural intervention of God in the form of an angel's visitation who struck him down to death, because he did not give God the glory. King Herod arrested some of the believers who belonged to the church. He intended to persecute them. He arrested James, the brother of John, and put him to death. Persecution pleased the Jews and so he proceeded to seize Peter also. Having imprisoned him, he intended to bring him out for public trial. However, Peter's life was saved by the visitation of an angel.

On one occasion, Herod arrayed in royal robes, delivered a public speech to his people. The people applauded shouting, *"This is the voice of a god, not of a man,"* (Acts 12:22). Immediately he was struck down to death by an angel, *"because Herod did not give praise to God,"* (Acts 12:23). Praising God and giving glory to Him, at least at this last moment, would have restrained God's hand of judgment on Herod. Humility brings praise. However, a man swollen with pride and puffed up with ego will meet his tragic end. The persecution, in fact, was carried out with the sole intention of stopping the spread of the Gospel. Nevertheless the story ends with a dramatic irony. *"But the word of God continued to increase and spread."* (Acts 12:24)

The prophet Habakkuk praises God in adverse circumstances; he sees violence and injustice among his own people. "*How could a just God tolerate wrong?*" he wondered. How could a just God allow His people to be punished by an evil nation, he complained. When God answers, it convinces him and fills him with joyful confidence. Evil may seem to dominate the earth, but it cannot be forever, he understood. God is silent only for a certain period, but not forever. There is a future and hope for every believer. Until then he will live by holding on to his faith in God.

"The righteous shall live by his faith."

[Habakkuk 2:4]

A believer should learn to close his eyes to the external circumstances and learn to rejoice in the strength of the Lord. There are circumstances that look contrary to our expectation. Can one praise God in such adverse moments? Habakkuk did praise God. His song of praise released him from the bondage of fear and confusion. He stopped complaining and started praising God and His ways. God is in perfect control of everything, now Habakkuk could profess boldly. He gained such confidence when he understood the plan of the Lord.

"You come out to deliver your people, to save your anointed one."

[Habakkuk 3:13]

Hence, words of praise flow spontaneously from a bruised heart; he had not seen a single bud on the tree. The tree is barren, devoid of leaves, branches and buds; yet he rejoices because the expected end is approaching nearer and nearer – the expected end to all trials and tribulations, persecutions and afflictions. The end to sorrows in other words, is a beginning to a new arrival, in the form of a revival. The pen may be empty without sheep today. God has promised to send His rain, which will revive the trees to blossom; it would fill the pen with His lost sheep. The prayer and praise of the persecuted Christians will move the hand of the Lord. He will send rain in its due season.

"Be glad then, you children of Zion, and rejoice in the Lord your God; For He has given you the former rain faithfully..."

[Joel 2:23]

God, therefore, wants to come forth in a manifestation of His glory and power in the form of revival. *For the earth will be filled with the knowledge and glory of the Lord, much as the waters cover the sea* (Habakkuk 2:14). The spiritual decline we see around us will change and soon we shall see revival. All nations will receive deliverance when the torrential outpour of latter rain is poured upon them. They will be released from the clutches of the devil.

Their plants and trees, their vineyards, their sheep and oxen had been devoured by worms; locusts and worms ate them. However, the Lord now made it clear by this remark:

"And I will restore... the years..."

[Joel 2:25]

Surely, God's promise gives us a hope and a future. All on a sudden, we are lifted from the hopeless state of despair. We remember Moses' word:

"Make us glad in proportion to the days, in which you have afflicted us, and to the years in which we have suffered evil."

[Psalm 90:15]

Captives from captivity are delivered miraculously by God's touch. Souls we find around, were painfully struggling to recover from their agonies of oppressive governments.

Bitter situations had created an atmosphere of mistrust and hatred. The good news is this: *"The government is upon His shoulders."* The prayers and praise of God's people alone will bring down the supernatural power of God. The enormous outpouring of His power and His Spirit can turn away the troubles that are coming upon nations.

Most of the religious meetings end up with a spiritual indulgence of the attainment of a high frenzied state of ecstasy. This outpouring equips one with power. With the God-vested power upon them, they should step out and set the captives free. The great longing of our God is to see lost souls delivered. Knowing His pulse beat, God's chosen people will start praising God for the power they are given. Much power is released in their praise. Birthing of spiritual children takes place very soon. The long stretch of a period of bondage to which they had been subjected to, will vanish in a trice. What a joyous return to breathe a fresh free breeze once again!

When the Lord brought back the captivity of Zion:

We were like those who dream. Then our mouth was filled with laughter; and our tongue with singing. Then they said among the nations, *"The Lord has done great things for them." The Lord has done great things for us, and we are glad."*

[Psalm 126: 1-3]

Joel prophesied:

"...whoever shall call on the name of the Lord shall be delivered..."

[Joel 2:32]

Zechariah prophesied:

"Many nations shall be joined to the Lord in that day."

[Zechariah 2:11]

Our prayer along with praise must go in accord with God's will. When God plants the seeds of new life in the womb of the church, calls are made to intercessory prayers, praise and worship. The Holy Spirit gives them the birth pangs. The intercessors and people who lead praise and worship realize that it is the time for the birth of a child, the church. The Holy Spirit is motivating them to spend more time in prayer. Under the inspiration of the Holy Spirit, God's chosen intercessors start to intercede for all. They feel the birth pangs and therefore they cry for a new era of a new generation.

Jesus Himself had to offer vehement cries with tears in the days of His flesh, to Him who was able to save Him from death. He learned obedience through all the sufferings He underwent. His obedience brought eternal salvation for all. We know our calling; we should move forward for what we are ordained. We are called to offer gifts and sacrifices for the sins of others. For, we can have compassion on those who are ignorant of God's judgment, and are going astray. To bring them back to His fold is the only desire of God.

There are people who were once spiritually enlightened; they have once tasted the heavenly gift; they were the partakers of the Holy Spirit; they have tasted the good word of God. In spite of all that, they backslide from their vision. The reasons for their faithlessness may be due to the love of money; or due to their love of people of the world who hate the principles of Jesus; or they could have lost their vision for which they had been called. These people might have been disappointed because they could not achieve their worldly goals, which they desired most in their hearts. They could not surrender their will to God.

These backsliders have lost their mission as well as their vision. *"…if they fall away, to renew them again to repentance, since they crucify again for themselves the Son of God, and put Him to an open shame."* (Hebrews 6:6)

To renew them to repentance, revival rain begins to flow. Blessed is the earth, which drinks in the rain that often comes upon it; blessed is the earth that bears herbs that are useful to mankind. In addition, at the same time, cursed is the land that bears thorns and briars whose end is to be rejected and burned forever. When the intercessors pray for their souls, God remembers them and saves those lost souls. For, our God is not an unjust God to forget their work; nor does He forget the labour of love which they have shown toward His name. With the Lord, there is mercy, and with Him is plenteous redemption. Once again, a river from Calvary flows forth with His precious and spotless blood – His blood carrying His love, grace and boundless mercy. Man has been faithless. But God is faithful unto the very end of man's life.

"For the Lord is good; His mercy is everlasting; and His truth endures to all generations," (Psalm 100:5). This is a song of praise for the Lord's faithfulness to His people, sung by David.

Houses are turned into houses of prayer for all nations. God raises new tabernacles to dwell in; He longs to prepare a host of souls for His kingdom. God's mighty wind and wave break through the land, sweeping away all demonic forces. The knowledge of His glory fills the land. Desolate lands rise up and shine forth for His glory.

The ruined cities are rebuilt for His glory. People will see the renewal everywhere. Thus says the Lord God:

"On the day that I cleanse you from all your iniquities, I will also enable you to dwell in the cities and the ruins shall be rebuilt. The desolate land shall be tilled instead of lying desolate in the sight of all who passes by. Therefore, they will say, 'This land that was desolate has become like the Garden of Eden; and the wasted, desolate, and ruined cities are now fortified and inhabited."

"Then the nations, which are left all around you, shall know that I, the Lord, have rebuilt the ruined places and planted what was desolate. I, the Lord have spoken it, and I will do it."

[Ezekiel 36:33-36.]

Abundant rain flows into the land and houses reviving everything it touches. People living in darkness cry out – repenting for their sins – *"Lord have mercy on us."*

There flows a river of spotless blood from His wounds. People fall slain under the mighty power of God. The evil spirits that had been tormenting the body leave as the river flows into the houses. Deliverance is secured in the bodies of those who fall prey to the power of evil spirits. The power of God shatters the power of unclean spirits.

The Holy Spirit has the mighty power to convict every sinful soul. People who slandered His name cry out unto the Lord. With a broken and repentant heart, they cry out for forgiveness of their sins. Conviction of sin comes back to them, since the Holy Spirit has come back upon them to revive their spirit. As Zechariah the prophet says,

"Not by might nor by power, but by My spirit, says the Lord Almighty."

[Zechariah 4:6]

We offer this prayer for nations with the firm faith that God's Holy Spirit shall surely work wonders.

You find no pleasure in the death of the wicked. You should forgive their wrongs and trespasses. Your mercy endures forever. You are a God of compassion. You are patient with every one of us. You do not want anyone to perish, but everyone to come to repentance. (II Peter 2:9)

Turn to us Lord, and we shall be turned and restored! Renew our days as of old!

[Lamentations 5:21]

We shall live forever under one kingdom, one king. The great vision is to see us all brought under one nation. They shall no longer be two nations, nor shall they be divided into two kingdoms.

People who were restored will no longer defile the land with their abominations; no longer will they bring any detestable thing into the land. Anything that was brought illegally shall leave the land. The Lord promises to sanctify people and their possessions. He accepts them as His own. He wants us to set up a tabernacle for Him, wherein He loves to dwell forever.

Indeed, the Lord will be our God, and we shall be His people. Once delivered from slavery we are cleansed of every transgression. We enjoy divine protection as our Lord God has made an everlasting covenant of peace with us. He will put His Spirit in us. He builds a new tabernacle for His own glory.

Christian faith is a kind of longing to serve humanity in a Christian way. God honours faith. God honours people who are faithful to Him. He empowers them to set the captives free.

We rise up on His Coming

With a new life;

We stand up with His majestic splendour.

It's something marvellous –

A renewal out of the ruins!

Out of the ruins, He rebuilds.

He needs only the ruins to rebuild

His glory He'll share it with none.

The barren lands lay waste

As far as our eyes could stretch

He looked for justice

He found injustice, instead.

He looked for righteousness

He found wickedness, instead.

Follies full of foibles were everywhere –

Life of people around

His own people played harlotry

Which He abhorred saying –

"The land is full of abomination

Which, Oh! Lord I detest!

Is the land of Judah

His chosen one, kept for destruction?

What then is the word of promise given to His remnant…?

"His mercy endureth forever"

"The Lord… is slow to anger and great in mercy."

"Hail Judah! Hail!"

Restoration is sure to bloom out of the remnant

Certain is your deliverance from bondage

His grace is ever flowing with just force

Filthy rags – filthy swine – foul smell

Out of that waste squalor rebel

A newborn baby was brought forth

A new fragrance pleasing to His heart